TWO-BY-FOUR

Stop Messing Around and Achieve Business Success

Alexandre Vézina

Alexandre Vézina
Entrepreneur/Consultant

Two-by-Four
Stop Messing Around and Achieve Business Success

By the same author:
Enfin les vraies affaires, Volume 1 (2016)
Enfin les vraies affaires, Volume 2 (2017)
Enfin les vraies affaires, Volume 3 (2018)
Tout simplement (co-author) (2018)
Deux-par-quatre, Arrête de niaiser si tu veux réussir en business
(2018)
Enfin les vraies affaires, L'intégrale (2019)
C'est de TA faute (2019)
Évolution (2020)
MARQUÉS AU FER ROUGE (2021)

Cover photo credit :   Karine Lévesque, Sens Image
Proofreading: Sébastien Hogue
Publisher: © Alexandre Vézina, 2022

For my children, Zachary and Zoé. Explore life, and stay curious. Always question the status quo (except when it's your parents who are talking to you). Listen to your intuition, and above all, be bold and ambitious in all of your endeavours.

I would also like to dedicate this book to my mentor, Charles René Lambert, who passed away one month before the publication of this book. Charles René, I see what an invaluable impact you had on my success as an entrepreneur-consultant, and I will always be grateful. It was a privilege to talk things over with you, and I already miss our regular discussions. I hope that, someday, I'll be able to have the kind of positive effect on other people's lives that you did. Thank you for everything.

BEFORE ANYTHING ELSE

Lyrics to Personal Jesus by Depeche Mode

Reach out and touch faith
Your own personal Jesus
Someone to hear your prayers
Someone who cares
Your own personal Jesus
Someone to hear your prayers
Someone who's there
Feeling unknown
And you're all alone
Flesh and bone
By the telephone
Lift up the receiver
I'll make you a believer
Take second best
Put me to the test
Things on your chest
You need to confess

I will deliver
You know I'm a forgiver
Reach out and touch faith

Reach out and touch faith
Your own personal Jesus
Someone to hear your prayers
Someone who cares
Your own personal Jesus
Someone to hear your prayers
Someone who's there

Stop complaining that other people don't understand you because they're not in your shoes. One of the most important lessons that entrepreneurs learn in my programs is this:

All entrepreneurs are in the same boat, and nearly all of them face the same challenges and situations.

So stop thinking that you're the only one in your situation.

Like many of you, I'm a lone wolf. But I have mentors in Québec and abroad, and I hire consultants who have specific expertise. My partners' strengths cover my own shortcomings, and the employees in my companies are much better than I would be in their respective roles.

To achieve success and avoid stagnation, we all need help from other people.

Get advice from people who've been there before, people who know more than you do about the challenges you're facing.

Above all, be humble enough to accept help from others, and choose the right people to work with.

INTRODUCTION

Another book? Again?

Yes, again. So many of the people who've read my trilogy of books for entrepreneurs, *Enfin les vraies affaires*, have given them a place of honour on their bedside tables, reading and rereading them to improve their positions as entrepreneurs.

On the other hand, some of my partners and clients have mentioned that the books are very lighthearted in tone. They say that their experience of interacting with me in person is completely different, particularly when I lock eyes with them and get down to real business.

It's true that I toned down my abrasive side in my first books, although they are still very practical and street smart (to quote Mathieu Dumont, director of Didacte).

In this new book, I want you to experience the kind of blunt advice I give to entrepreneurs regularly, in order to spur them to action.

To make it authentic, bold and filter-free, I decided to

write it in just 24 hours, spread out over six weeks. No more, no less.

Before you continue reading, however, a word of caution:

At some point, as you're reading along, I'm probably going to make you angry. And that's good.

You'll think to yourself, "Alex, you're pissing me off, but you're totally right. You aimed well with that two-by-four, and it hit me square in the face again. But you won't get me next time, because I'm going to start doing things differently, for my own personal and professional growth."

Emotions make people act, as my esteemed colleague Alan Weiss says.

I'm sure you'll experience a few as you read.

In short, this book directly reflects the way I keep my business promise: to improve the situation of entrepreneurs, with no kid gloves and no beating around the bush.

If anyone thinks I'm too direct, too bad for them. They can go play with the fairies and unicorns in the land of Everything-is-Beautiful-and-Fine. Getting smacked with a two-by-four is never pleasant. But it's memorable, and I guarantee that you'll be motivated to improve in order to keep it from happening again.

Here's a little secret: I wrote this book for myself, not just for other people. I wish someone else had written it first, and given it to me when I was just starting out in my career. If they had, I would be 15 years ahead of where I am now.

Happy reading.

September 2018

STOP FOOLING AROUND AND PICK UP THE PHONE

The era of emails, chats and texting has made us timid and weak.

Many entrepreneurs and employees use these communication tools to avoid difficult conversations. It's easier to write to someone to tell them that they have to pay their $15,000 bill than it is to say it out loud.

You're afraid to call your client to ask for the money they owe you. And yet you're not robbing them, the contract was completed successfully.

Inversely, most entrepreneurs are scared to talk to potential customers over the phone. They'd rather delegate that task to companies that provide phone prospecting services, or just skip it entirely.

Who is best placed to represent your company? You and your employees, or an external sales representative who doesn't understand what you do, reading a script like a robot?

Is that the image you want to project?

Seriously, the problem here is your fear of rejection and conflict.

If you don't pick up the phone, nothing is ever going to happen. Then you'll end up lying to yourself, calling yourself unlucky because you haven't been as successful as you hoped to be.

In my opinion, there's no such thing as luck. There are only the opportunities that we make for ourselves. Period. You have to make your own luck by picking up the phone and daring to call.

I humbly admit that I have sometimes been weak and scared too.

Like most people, I absolutely despise calling complete strangers to try and sell them something. No one likes getting "no" for an answer. Unfortunately, it's a necessary evil if you want to build a wider customer base and support the growth of your business.

Being an entrepreneur means constantly getting "no" for an answer. I'm sure you've already noticed that.

Social media and email also make us vulnerable, both in terms of our regular customers and our potential customers. You have no control over the timing or efficacy of the reply, or whether or not your target will be there at your chosen moment. And with all the other distractions in their frenzied lives, they may well forget all about you.

You wait patiently for them to get back to you, and it so seldom happens.

For businesses, waiting is a silent killer.

The truth is, while it's very easy to ignore an email, it's not as easy to hang up on someone. Remember, people tend to be just as afraid of refusing something or rejecting someone to avoid conflict as you are of hearing "no."

Don't take refusals and rejection personally. It's nothing personal, it's just business

You can use email for announcing your intentions and sparking interest in your business, or to "warm up your prospect." But for the next step, you have to start with picking up the phone. If you don't, you'll be just like so many other entrepreneurs, waiting patiently for someone else to make the first move. Which, by the way, is weak and lazy.

You have to learn to be resilient, and stop taking rejection as a personal affront.

A "no" can often be an opportunity to negotiate, and an additional challenge.

MY FIRST WHACKS

I would like to humbly tell you about the first entrepreneurial two-by-four whack I ever received. I've never told this story before.

It was 2006. I had just finished an internship in process improvement with the government of Québec, and I had turned down the opportunity to extend it into a student job for the summer. Continue doing the same job for half the salary? No thanks!

I was picky about the kind of student job I wanted, since it would be temporary. I'd started working and making money at age 15, so I had a nice little nest egg already.

I went through a rigorous hiring process at Location Sauvageau in Québec City. During the second interview, the director asked me, "What are your hobbies?"

"I play music, and I have a music creation business," I replied.

He looked at me skeptically, then continued:

"Does your business earn you a living?"

"No, we're just starting out."

"Well, either you're extremely brilliant and your business manages itself and generates sufficient income, or what you have is an entrepreneurial project. If that's the case, don't try to tell me that you have a business if you aren't generating sufficient income."

They offered me the job, and I turned it down because of the director's comment. He had pissed me off.

Hearing the truth shook me up. But he was right. I had bragged to the director of a respectable company, and in return he had given me a priceless gift: a question that was a whack from a two-by-four.

I needed to create businesses that would quickly become self-sustaining with little operational intervention on my part, and I needed to try and keep my own living wage separate to avoid exposing myself to too much risk.

I had discovered my quest: I would learn to do that.

That whack changed my whole way of thinking and helped me get to where I am now.

Sometimes people don't tell us what we *want* to hear, they tell us what we *need* to hear.

ASSERTIONS AND CONSISTENCY

In a recent conversation, my communications and public relations advisor, David Couturier, said to me, "You know, Alex, in every single one of your projects, your biggest challenge is making sure that what you say (in your books, trainings, conferences, newsletters, blog posts, etc.) is consistent with what you do. Because the more declarations you make, the more likely it is that someone will throw your contradictions right back in your face."

It's true. The more we assert and reveal ourselves, the more we open ourselves to attacks from others, because we're contradicting their beliefs and ideas.

I recently offended someone in my network with my blog post, *Je ne suis pas un coach.* He told me that "the era of the whip is over," and that after reading my post, he no longer plans to attend any of my future book launches.

Too bad for him. I don't have any time to waste

on someone like that who isn't a potential customer or a good source of referrals, and whose personality clashes with mine (despite my best efforts). Let's be honest: I was a threat to his business.

Next.

In my opinion, being truly yourself is an extremely powerful way of showing uniqueness and making the world a better place, without worrying about hiding who you are from others.

We can't please everyone anyway.

It's hard to have a positive impact on other people's lives if you don't know who you truly are.

Being in the public eye increases your self-confidence, because you're not worried about hiding anything.

You'll attract the right customers, and drive away the others[1].

Sophie, an entrepreneur who attended one of my workshops, told me she didn't have the personality type required to "smack people with two-by-fours like Alexandre Vézina."

"That's not the goal, Sophie," I said. "However, I'm convinced that you're much more direct in person than in writing, and that you have the courage to say things directly to your customers without writing them down."

"That's true, I do!"

"So stop messing around and start sharing those thoughts on social media and in your emails. Basically, just be more yourself in all your communications."

Since then, Sophie has decided to be even more genuine in her conversations, distinguishing her company from all the bland, monotonous businesses out there. Now she'll attract even more customers, and they'll be a better fit for her.

Stop tiptoeing around whenever you communicate. Be yourself and say what you mean, damn it!

I'LL BE DEAD AT 50

June 2008

I was playing guitar in my apartment in Saint-Anselme, Bellechasse when the phone rang. My parents' phone number popped up on the screen.

"Hi, Mom."

"Hello, Le Gars." (Yeah, my family nickname was "the Guy." I assure you, it was better than the ones my two sisters were given…) "I just got my test results, and I have cancer that has already spread…"

"How long do you have?"

"What do you mean, Le Gars?"

"How long do you have left to live?"

"Why are you asking me that?"

"Because the tone of your voice makes me think I can guess the answer."

"Alex, please don't tell your sisters yet, but the doctors

told me they can't eradicate the disease, they can only try to ease the pain. They say I have about a year left to live."

During that year, I composed an entire album of music that I never released, for no real reason. More importantly, I made a list of everything I wanted to accomplish professionally, personally and with my family.

I identified my purpose in life, explored my skills and outlined my strategy, leaving some leeway in terms of choosing which tactics to use to reach each milestone.

For example, I have to be a millionaire before I turn 36. I want to give a million dollars to a non-profit organization before I turn 40. I want to have 25% ownership in a professional hockey team by age 45. I want to help over a million entrepreneurs worldwide improve their lives, and I want to write 50 books. All this, while owning multiple businesses so that I can learn faster, and, most importantly of all, before I turn 50, since that was the age at which my mother passed away on May 16, 2009.

Even though I will probably live longer than that, everything I do is in line with meeting these goals. Afterwards, I'll be even more ambitious.

All too often, we don't decide to act until we're faced with a challenge or a disease.

What are you waiting for?

When your objective is clear, it's much easier to make choices, identify the right decisions and, most importantly, think strategically.

Do you have a clear idea of what you want to accomplish?

STOP FOOLING AROUND AND DO IT

I've been putting off a certain task for at least a year: I need to write a content block of nine weeks of emails for one of my companies, the Clinique d'Accompagnement Entrepreneurial du Québec (CAEQ).

And this coming from an entrepreneur who writes books!

But the structure is simple and the content has been chosen. All I have to do is take the time to write the text.

Whenever I set time aside to complete this task, I end up doing something else. Every distraction that pops up is more appealing. I'm putting it off again to write this chapter!

When we spend too much time thinking about a task, our brains play a dirty trick: they immobilize us, and come up with a thousand and one ways to keep us from doing it.

When we get stuck like that, we also deplete an important resource: our brain juice.

That's right! If we don't do it right away, we'll continue to consider it from time to time until it's too late and we've become overwhelmed by the countless items that have accumulated on our to-do lists.

We have to learn to turn our brains off from time to time so we can switch to "execution" mode.

So, in this chapter, I'm whacking myself with the two-by-four.

"Come on, Alex, whenever you're unmotivated by a task and it's something you have to do it yourself, QUIT FOOLING AROUND AND JUST DO IT."

Just do it, and move on to the next task.

You can have fun writing books later.

And if you're in the same boat, dear reader, stop reading this book and GO DO THE DAMN TASK that you've left hanging for too long.

THE COBBLER ALWAYS WEARS THE WORST SHOES

T he title says it all, doesn't it?

I can tell you're already rolling your eyes, pursing your lips, and thinking, "Yeah, yeah, I know."

A lot of entrepreneurs and professionals are shoemakers in cheap shoes:

The website designer without a functional website.

The accountant whose accounts aren't up to date.

The marketing specialist who has no marketing presence.

The financial planner with no money to invest.

The landscaper with the gravel driveway.

The coach who dispenses advice that he himself

doesn't follow.

The owner of a retail business who doesn't buy her own goods.

The caterer who doesn't eat his own food.

The high-end German car salesman driving a Korean car.

The list goes on…

We justify our actions by saying that it's because we put the customer first.

Bullshit.

"Do as I say, not as I do" is the best way to get ditched by a customer or employee, and reveals a complete lack of consistency between what you do and what you say.

Did you know that this kind of behaviour can also affect your self-confidence?

Does this apply to you?

It's time to start being professional and consistent, wouldn't you say?

I'M RICH

It's early July, the sun is shining, and I've got $100,000 in my bank account. There's no financial stress whatsoever on the horizon. To maintain my reputation as a good customer, I quickly pay off all our suppliers, even though I only just received their invoices. I don't wait until the due date to send them their cheques, and I don't make any late payments.

By mid-August, the weather is still great, but there's no more money in the company's coffers. Every day at noon, I hurry to the post office, hoping that we've received a check that will keep us going for a few more days. I track all outstanding accounts receivable, but every single administrative officer seems to be on vacation, delaying the payment process. I'm frustrated, and I have no idea how we'll get through the end of the month with all the bills we have to pay.

Uh-oh, and I forgot to set a little money aside for myself...
  Apart from my mentor at the time, no one in my circle was aware of the situation. I knew it was temporary, but I still had to get through it.

I don't learn very quickly in some situations. Like this one. It was the second time something like this had happened. The first was during my time at BLV Transport, and the second occurred while I was working as a consultant . Like so many entrepreneurs, I'd managed my cash flow poorly.

I had made the mistake of paying some suppliers too quickly, that is to say as soon as I received the invoice, even though they had given me 30 days to pay. At the same time, many of my customers were waiting 30, 60 and even over 90 days to make their payments, for no good reason in my opinion.

I had been counting on the good faith of my customers, forgetting that due to summer vacations and, in some cases, seasonal declines in work, it was a challenging time for many companies and organizations.

You don't need a degree in finance to understand why it caused a liquidity crisis.

I can tell you one thing for sure: In high-stress situations like this one, you'll come up with some creative financial gymnastics in a hurry to make money appear.

Fighting for the survival of your business has to be temporary. How can you plan the future and growth of your business with the sword of Damocles hanging over your head?

That's why I always tell my clients to maintain a margin of financial flexibility in terms of access to liquidity, and to constantly be increasing their credit lines. It's better to ask when you don't actually need it, right?

Monitor your numbers regularly, organize things to keep them up to date, go after your money and, most importantly, plan your payments accordingly.

A

COUNTERINTUITIVE
TIP

Do you own a company that's unprofitable, no longer motivates you, offers uneven quality, has uncommitted employees, and provides products or services in order to "survive" rather than thrive, with suboptimal customers who only want to spend as little as possible?

If your answer is "yes," you absolutely have to reduce your company's size and obligations in order to spur growth.

I have made this recommendation several times since starting out as an entrepreneur-consultant.

Unfortunately, entrepreneurs tend to wait until they're running on empty and have no other choice before taking action.

Every year, you need to play the janitor: Take out the trash that's sapping your energy and brain juice and keeping your company from becoming successful.

To be successful, you absolutely have to make difficult decisions that can sometimes be emotional.

"I'll give him one more chance. He was my very first employee, and he helped get me where I am today."

So what?

There's only one questions that matters: Can he help you move forward in your chosen direction?

No? Then too bad, cut him loose.

Every year, you have to analyze your products and services, as well as those of your customers, employees, partners, suppliers, contacts, and any opportunities waiting for follow-up, as well as any ongoing projects, to ensure that they are aligned with your current vision.

Get rid of anything that won't help you make progress in each of the above categories, and fill the new openings with promising new elements that support the direction you've decided to take. Your cuts should represent 15%.

Why 15%?

Let's call it the normal distribution of entrepreneurship: 15% of what you and your customers do is excellent, 70% is okay, and the remaining 15% just drags you down. Get rid of that last 15%, or whatever keeps you from making progress.

How do you get rid of it?

It's easy:

Turn down opportunities by explaining why you're refusing and specifying the type of opportunity that reflects your vision. The next time that contact offers you an opportunity, it will be in alignment with your goals[3].

Find new roles for employees who no longer fit into your current corporate culture, or simply let them go.

Suggest alternatives from your competitors to any of your customers who are no longer ideal, or increase your rates significantly to encourage them to go elsewhere.

Find new suppliers and negotiate with your old ones.

Eliminate development projects that are no longer consistent with your objectives.

Eliminate products in decline.

The list goes on...

Don't make the mistake of thinking that maintaining all the resources you needed in the past is a good strategy for reaching your future destination.

You should mow your lawn whenever the grass gets too long and the weeds appear.

The same goes for your company.

HIT A DEAD END?

I was in a meeting with one of my clients, Marie-Josée Deschênes, an architect and entrepreneur specializing in historical buildings. She was frustrated: Two of her five employees had just handed in their notice, effective almost immediately.

"Alex, I have no idea how to continue running my business under these conditions. I've hit a dead end."

"First off, as long as you're still there, everything can keep going. Everyone is replaceable, and if you're still around there's hope. You're the cornerstone of your business, right? You, not your employees. Secondly, I think this is an incredible opportunity for you."

"What do you mean?"

"For years now, I've been telling you to focus exclusively on projects in the historical preservation niche. Now you won't have to find lots of small contracts to pay your employees' salaries. You can focus all your prospecting efforts on projects that you're really passionate about."

We all get to a point where we feel like we've hit a dead end with our businesses. It's normal to have a bad day and feel discouraged. When it happens, give yourself a moment, then roll up your sleeves.

But continuing to mope around two weeks later is weak, fearful and selfish.

It's weak because giving up is the easy way out, fearful because you're trying to curl up and hide, and selfish because you think you're the only one affected by the situation, forgetting your business's stakeholders (customers, employees, suppliers, creditors, etc.).

Change your perspective. A dead end is a new challenge to face. That's all.

I often ask my clients, "Do you feel like you've tried everything possible to overcome, bypass or break through this roadblock?"

They rarely say "yes."

Ask yourself these questions when faced with a daunting challenge:

Do I know anyone who has been through this kind of ordeal before?

Do I know anyone who can give me a little extra help with this? A specialist, perhaps?

Am I forcing my way down a path that really is impassable? If so, can I turn back and try another one instead?

If you think that entrepreneurship is always smooth

sailing, you're wrong. Once you've jumped in with both feet, it's more like swimming for your life, with a dozen sharks circling you every second of the day.

Be resilient. It can be exciting with the right attitude, because true leaders are forged by adversity, not simplicity.

In closing, here's a quote from *Le Cid* by Corneille: "To win without risk is to triumph without glory."

WHAT TO DO WHEN THINGS GO WRONG

I am often approached by struggling entrepreneurs looking for help. I tell them that my expertise lies in business growth, not business recovery.

However, I always take 15 minutes to tell them the following, based on my own experience.

"If you have loans, request a payment moratorium immediately."

A payment moratorium is a given time period during which you only pay the interest on your loans, not the principal. Payments on the principal are deferred. This tip can help reduce the strain of your financial obligations. You can make the same request for home mortgage payments if you are in a difficult personal situation.

"If you owe the government money for taxes collected, employee payroll deductions or corporate taxes, call an agent to make payment arrangements immediately. You can spread your payments out over a maximum of one year. And do it now, instead of just staring at your phone or your computer."

You absolutely have to be proactive instead of sitting around being reactive.

Being proactive means:

Responding to every request you receive quickly.

Answering all emails and calls.

Honouring your commitments.

Being honest with yourself about your situation.

Picking up the phone and calling people in your network who can send work your way.

Participating in different networking activities.

Going to the places where your potential customers are.

Increasing your marketing efforts.

Getting out and meeting potential customers.

Facilitating and commenting on social media posts.

The list goes on...

These tips are also essential for developing businesses. So stop procrastinating, and start putting them into practice.

ENTREPRENEURIAL JEALOUSY

I have to admit, I'm jealous of some of those pseudo-experts you see online, with their large followings and credibility among certain aspiring entrepreneurs. The internet and Facebook are swimming in pseudo-experts who copy their magic recipes from other self-proclaimed gurus. The worst part is that, for a few of them, it actually works. It bugs me to see entrepreneurs get sucked into their flim-flam when they would be much better served by my businesses, and the operating models I've developed over time based on first-hand experience.

Many entrepreneurs hang on their every word, as if they were prophets announcing the coming of a new god who calculates value in conversion rates and cost-per-click. In reality, the only thing these "experts" have succeeded at is a mastery of social media, and sometimes cheating.[4].

Every time I think about it, I want someone to slap me in the face. Hence this chapter.

There will always be people who are more successful that you are, or at least appear to be. They'll have more money, a bigger house, a more luxurious car, newer electronic gadgets, better skills, they'll look happier (although it's often just a misleading front on social media, designed to hide a reality that's quite different…), and so on.

Good for them.

Jealousy does nothing but distract you by diverting your attention to trivial matters. It has nothing positive to offer, either personally or professionally. It throws you off balance by casting doubt on what you do and how you do it, and undermines your self-confidence.

You alone are responsible for the energy you spend on this emotion. Remember what Eleanor Roosevelt once said: "No one can make you feel inferior without your consent."

Reread this chapter whenever you start to feel jealousy setting in.

Stays focused on your life and business goals, and help others achieve theirs.

11:15 P.M.

Once again, I've just wasted (spent) 30 minutes of my life doing nothing on Facebook. I tell myself that I'm gathering information about various things, when what actually happens is:

I get hooked by advertisements from pseudo-experts promising to teach me how to make money effortlessly in their webinar or "funnel," because Facebook knows that I'm an entrepreneur.

My news feed is full of holiday pictures of people I don't care about. I haven't spoken with them in 15 years (or more), and with any luck, I won't have to for the next 15 either.

Parents share videos of their children instead of just enjoying the moment themselves: "Why keep this to myself when I can let the whole world experience it at the same time via live broadcast if I watch it through my phone?"

People post anything and everything without the slightest embarrassment, and they "tag" other people who never wanted any part of it.

Some people post information about lost cats and dogs that get shared 50 times, even though the missing animal has been back home for a week.

Far too many people think they're ready for the Supreme Court, even though a sardine has better judgment than they do.

I get it that people like sharing important moments in their lives. Like a video of a monkey flipping off zoo visitors, for example.

But once again, let's be honest here: A lot of people have built a life or career for themselves on social media, but I'm afraid they turn out to be phonies when you talk to them face to face. As soon as an interaction doesn't fit into their posting schedule, it becomes obvious that they're only this week's empty trend, and they topple off their ephemeral, star-studded pedestals. Oops! Three years down the line, emails sent to them will bounce back and their number will be disconnected, even though they spent a fortune to show their audience that anyone can make a living doing what they love and generate a steady income, even from a beach on the other side of the world.

Those experts end up having to beg on their hands and knees for some slave driver to assign them a cubicle in an office building. The security guard at the door is a constant reminder that they are now prisoners of a new kind of freedom, based on the credit that, unfortunately, they now have to repay with tenfold interest.

This new platform can provide visibility for certain people, but it's a waste of time for those who want to accomplish something real without focusing solely on appearances.

There's a difference between doing business online and using social media as a means of sharing relevant information, and sitting around watching cat videos.

The things people end up doing to feel alive and distract themselves from reality can be truly absurd. It's much easier to waste 30 minutes online than it is to do something productive with the same amount of time.

Get out your calculator: 30 minutes a day, 365 days a year... that's 182.5 hours a year!

That's almost 23 eight-hour work days.

Are you a professional time-waster?

P.S. It's now 11:30 p.m. One more chapter down!

THE COMPETITION IS NOT YOUR WORST ENEMY

Have you become your own worst enemy?

Do you check your email and social media countless times a day?

Do you bother someone else as soon as you have a question?

Do you think multitasking makes you more productive?

Do you send messages outside of normal office hours?

Do you start your day not knowing which task to tackle first?

We often trigger our own downfalls. We let other

people and the technology that surrounds us interrupt our work, distracting us from the basics and pulling our focus.

Emails, smartphones, text messages and social media have made us slaves to interruptions, and we have only ourselves to blame.

Not to say that I'm anti-technology! If anything, the opposite is true.

But we have to decide how we're going to use technology, and the kind of interruptions we're willing to accept.

So what can you do to reduce the number of daily interruptions?

There are lots of time management techniques available out there, but you need to figure out what works for you. We're all different, and unfortunately there isn't a single strategy that is 100% suitable for everyone's needs and working style.

These are the habits that work for me:

Alerts: I've turned off all audible alerts on my phone and smartwatch, because as soon as I hear them, I tend to look, even if I'm in the middle of a conversation with someone. It isn't very professional.

Email: I check and answer my emails once an hour when I'm in the office. Or else I reply during my lunch break, or at the end of the day.

Phone: I turn off my phone whenever I'm working on an important task that requires concentration, or when I'm meeting with clients. I usually make calls while on the road, or at the end of the day. Unless it's from one of my partners, I don't answer calls before 8:00 a.m. or after 5:00 p.m. Instead, I delegate that task to my favourite assistant: my voicemail.

Social media: I start my day by catching up on my social media alerts and interacting on those platforms. I take advantage of my lunch break and late afternoon to do it again. I also use in-between times and breaks between meetings to make sure that there haven't been any posts that require my immediate attention.

I check emails and social media one last time after my kids are in bed, and I only reply if there's something that can't wait until morning.

Weekends: All right, yes, I check my email and social media three times a day over the weekend. But I don't have my phone on me all the time, and I sometimes even leave it at home when I'm out with my family.

Don't let yourself be caught up in the endless whirl. Set up a structure that will help you create more effective habits.

Be disciplined, and stick to it.

STOP GETTING ADVICE FROM FRIENDS AND FAMILY

Your friends and family aren't your strategic business development advisers, far from it. Especially if they aren't entrepreneurs themselves. Any advice they give you will be in their own best interest more than in yours.

Don't get me wrong, they're happy for you. But your worries and triumphs will probably bore them to tears. Your excitement may even cause jealousy, and lead to comments like these:

"We can't all make a living doing what we love the way you do."

"We already know you can do whatever you want

because you're the boss."

An entrepreneur is like a pirate, out there searching for the treasures that everyone else can only dream of.

We have to accept that we're different from everybody else.

So share your concerns and triumphs with other entrepreneurs, who can actually benefit from them. There's a reason why business mentoring is so popular these days.

We all need someone to listen to us and ask us questions, and we need people who can answer our questions directly and won't pass the buck every time.

Stop wasting your breath on the wrong people.

"All right, but Alex, can't I talk to my spouse about it?"

Umm, well…

I have to admit that there's no easy answer to that question. So I asked Audrey, my wife.

And you should ask your spouse too, so you can get a straight answer and tailor your discussions accordingly.

Based on personal experience, I recommend briefly sharing your accomplishments and successes with your partner, and avoiding discussions about the major difficulties and concerns you encounter.

The reason is simple: In my opinion, there's nothing constructive about putting your spouse through extra stress. In general, their suggestions and comments won't do anything to improve your difficult situation because, as I mentioned above, despite their best intentions they are terrible listeners and terrible advisors. They'll talk about their own discomfort with the problem instead of actually helping you solve it.

"I told you so."

"Why don't you just get a regular job?"

"Do we have any money left?"

"What? You used the house as collateral?"

I also recommend filtering out sensitive information during your discussions, particularly when it comes to financial matters and the actual risks you take. Remember that we all have different comfort levels when it comes to risk.

In short, establish clear limits on how much influence your marital relationship has on your business, explain them to your better half and ask for their understanding.

Who will you talk to about your business from now on?

Only the trusted advisers, fellow entrepreneurs and mentors who can really help you.

TALKING THROUGH YOUR HAT

I was speaking with a commercial account manager from a financial institution in Québec. He had read my trilogy, Enfin les vraies affaires, and he had this to say:

"Mr. Vézina, I already know pretty much everything you've written in your books. I could have written them myself!"

If you're guessing that I was trying not to laugh, you're right.

"Great! In that case, I have two questions for you. First, do you follow all my tips? Probably not, since you're not an entrepreneur. And second, why didn't you write those books yourself?"

I admit it was a little bit rude, and that I took mischievous pleasure in knocking someone down to size. After all, he saw himself as a total rock star of financing and consulting for entrepreneurs, even though he'd never actually taken those kinds of risks himself.

I'm not saying he isn't excellent at what he does. But it's arrogant and presumptuous to pretend you know the game because you're familiar with the theory.

Here in Québec, we call that "talking through your hat."

To know and not to do is not to know. – Leo Buscaglia

Being aware of something and actually knowing it are not quite the same.

You have to use what you've learned to solidify it and turn it into a new business instinct. If you don't, you're wasted valuable time learning things that do nothing for you besides making you sound smarter when you talk.

Also, make sure you prioritize advice from people with experience over tips from those who only have theory.

After all, success is measured by results.

THERE ARE NO SPEED LIMITS

I can be pretty lazy sometimes.

I procrastinate a little before diving into less-exciting tasks. I read emails several times before replying, keep potential clients waiting, and ignore calls or take a while to return them after listening to my voicemail.

But all of those habits hurt my business. I should be striking while the iron is hot.

I've lost several hundreds of thousands of dollars by acting this way.

One of my mentors, Alan Weiss, taught me that, in the world we live in, "speed is everything."

For once, no speed limits have been set by governmental authorities. You bear sole responsibility for your driving and your vehicle's potential.

I am fully aware that we all have differing cruising speeds. But if you want to boost the success of your business, you have to learn to move faster.

So, how long do you take to:

Reply to your emails?

Submit a business proposal to a customer?

Schedule a meeting?

Return calls?

Greet a customer when they come into your store?

Respond to a complaint?

Ship an online order?

Follow up on your agreements?

Your response time can often be a major asset.

Being quick in these situations shows your professionalism and gives your clients a preview of the level of service your company provides.

Assuming that you offer top quality goods and services, has a customer ever complained because you were too fast?

Think about it for a minute.

Work on getting faster. Add a jetpack to your turtle shell.

ARE YOU ILLITERATE?

You are about to make a presentation to a potential customer that could take your business to the next level. You plug in the projector to start your pitch... and your presentation doesn't appear on screen.

You check your settings, and try making a few adjustments. Still nothing.

Five minutes later, you give up. You apologize for wasting your audience's valuable time with this amateurish mistake, and move your tablet closer to your audience so that they can at least attempt to read the tiny font of your planned presentation.

I'm sure that you've either been in a situation like this one or experienced it as a client.

Whenever you have to tell someone that you don't understand how your smartphone works, you don't know how to change your email settings, you can't "copy-paste" on your tablet, or you aren't able to connect a projector to a computer or use a remote control, you're diminishing your value.

You're projecting an image of incompetence.

Are you stuck in the previous century?

These are the kinds of problems that digital illiterates or "computosaurs" have to face.

These days, you have to at least learn to effectively use your own electronic equipment, or have a fairly advanced knowledge of how it works.

I can understand that we all have things to learn and discover when it comes to technology, since it evolves so quickly. But please, find someone quickly who can help you master the tools, devices and applications you use on a regular basis.

Don't let digital incompetence leave you powerless and undermine your self-confidence.

The same goes for your employees.

Welcome to the 21st century.

SHUT YOUR TRAP

This happened some time ago. I was in a meeting with Jean, a construction contractor, when he received a call from one of his clients.

"Alex, I absolutely have to take this. But you can stay here in the office," he told me, quickly answering the call.

I told him to go ahead.

To my astonishment, what was supposed to be a short call dragged on and on.

BLA BLA BLA, until the call ended (finally).

When at long last he hung up, I gave him one of my trademark smirks.

"What's wrong, Alex?"

"That conversation could have been over in 30 seconds. Instead you took five minutes to provide details to your client that weren't important, and that he probably didn't understand."

Jean was obviously taken aback by what I'd said.

"You're absolutely right. I was just thinking out loud, trying to explain why I handled the situation by moving a wall to comply with the current standards…"

"And you may have even cast a shadow of doubt in your client's mind, since you didn't sound very confident about the solution you found."

"In that case, I'm glad you were here when I took the call. You've just helped me realize that I do that with all my clients, employees and partners. No wonder I run out of time every day…"

Jean understood immediately that he could save time and, above all, project the image of a confident entrepreneur in his consultations with his clients. In short, reassure his customers instead of worrying them.

I used to waste my breath like that, so I know what I'm talking about.

A few months ago, I was invited to a meeting with economic development partners to talk about one of my entrepreneurship programs. I'd been explaining the unique nature of the program for five minutes when one of the decision-makers in the room suddenly stopped me.

"You're preaching to the choir, Alex! Tell us HOW we can get a group started as quickly as possible, instead of focusing on the logic behind this kind of program."

I froze for a few seconds, surprised by the accuracy of the comment.

I had launched straight into my sales pitch, without asking what my audience was hoping to learn. Why? I had gotten into the habit of always presenting the program in the same way, like playing a video. I'd pressed the *replay* button, focusing on MY methodology instead of being agile and adapting my presentation to my audience. *Once again, I was talking too much.*

I was thinking about MYSELF instead of my CLIENTS.

Have you ever noticed that in business?

We often talk too much, for one reason or other. These reasons have more to do with reassuring OURSELVES than with persuading OTHERS.

Keep this in mind during future interactions with your clients, prospects and partners.

Shake up your old habits, find out what your audience wants, and be brief.

And above all, stop trying to sell to people who have already bought what you're selling.

Too much talk is bad for your business.

SET AN EXAMPLE[5]

"**M**y employees just don't get it. I've told them time and time again to use the parking spaces in back, and leave the ones in front of the store for the customers."

"Okay, but you need to set the example. Instead, you have a space reserved for yourself right in front of the window."

Bam! Right in the face.

By now you've probably guessed that I love it when this kind of thing happens.

We're always complaining about employees and co-workers who don't follow the company rules and procedures we've set up, when we're the first to ignore them.

For example:

You say "no discounts," but then you lower the price as soon as someone starts bargaining.

You talk about how you want your employees to be independent, but you always take over for them when clients are present.

You insist that every customer must pay before leaving with their merchandise, but you make exceptions all the time.

Observing the official working hours is supposedly important, and yet you're always the last to arrive.

You ask your employees to be flexible and willing to replace a colleague on short notice, but you aren't flexible yourself.

Your employees have several tasks they're supposed to perform when there are a lot of customers, but you don't even help them on the floor.

"Yes, but I'm the boss."

That's the point. Your employees will follow your lead.

How do you expect people to take what you say seriously when your behaviour towards them is inconsistent?

Whenever you give any kind of instructions to one of your employees, ALWAYS make sure you're doing it yourself. That's what we call being a leader.

A leader sets the example under all circumstances.

If you don't, it's not other people who are the problem, it's you. Even if you only park your car out front for two minutes.

Are you a leader, or are you just faking it?

WHY, WHY, WHY...

Every parent knows that children almost always ask "why?" when you give them a task with no explanation.

The same holds true for your employees. How can you expect them to perform a task properly if they don't understand why they should use the technique you've given them?

It's all too easy to overlook this step. Then we end up frustrated when employees don't do their job well.

But really, it's our fault.

As entrepreneurs, it's our responsibility to clearly explain to the entire team why a task must be performed in a specific way.

Jacques, a client of mine who runs a manufacturing company, learned this the hard way.

"Alex, I'm facing some quality issues at the moment, and I'm experiencing serious raw material losses. I've been working with the same employees for ages, and this is the first time something like this has happened."

"To fix the issue, it's important to identify the problem's underlying cause. When did you first begin noticing these problems?"

"About a year ago, after I hired a new production supervisor. He doesn't follow instructions or procedures, and he's made some changes on the assembly line to improve performance at each station."

"Bingo! He's probably an amateur trying to get continuous improvement."

"What?

"Some people instinctively try to reinvent the wheel because they want to improve the system. While this might look great on paper, it can be counterproductive when the proposed improvements have been thought out and implemented from a micro, rather than a macro, perspective. In other words, the supervisor has improved a few workstations at the expense of the entire assembly line."

"Oh my God… It all makes sense now. By giving him a free hand, I almost let him run my company into the ground."

Before making any changes to a system that works, it's important to assess whether those changes will have a positive impact on the overall production process, or a toxic one. Don't fall into the trap of evaluating efficiency station by station.

You also have to explain to your supervisors and employees why they need to operate the system the way they were trained to, and submit any potential improvements for your approval before making changes. This will help counter the effects of short-sightedness.

If you want employees to perform their tasks properly, it's your job to clarify the bigger picture for each of them by explaining exactly why they have to follow your decisions and procedures.

A STRIPTEASE
ALWAYS LEAVES
AN IMPRESSION

I was talking with Caroline recently. She's a fashion entrepreneur, and I'd really love to help her take her business to the next level. With so much on my plate, I'm not really taking on new clients for individual coaching outside of my group programs for entrepreneurs these days. Also, I had been charging $425 an hour, which I wasn't quite comfortable with, even though my clients insisted that it was worth it.

So I suggested that she sign up for one of my group programs, or the Clinique d'Accompagnement Entrepreneurial (Entrepreneurship Coaching Clinic), so we could work together every week online.

"No, Alex," she said. "I need more. I want to work closely with you and have direct access to your expertise."

"Let me think about it, Caroline. I'll get back to you next

week."

Any sane consultant would have immediately jumped at the opportunity. Not me.

I had a card up my sleeve, something I had never mentioned. Until now.

Every year, I offer unlimited access to everything I do to a select number of clients. At the end of that year, I evaluate the impact my coaching has had, and I charge accordingly. I don't make the offer lightly, since that kind of commitment is demanding and requires so much energy on my part.

But remember, Caroline was already eager to work with me and had asked me to make her another kind of offer.

In this kind of situation, I do what I like to call an "entrepreneurial striptease."

Definition of the word "striptease": *A striptease is an erotic or exotic dance in which the performer gradually undresses, either partly or completely, in a seductive and sexually suggestive manner. (Source: Wikipedia)*

I define "entrepreneurial striptease" as the art of stimulating interest in your business in order to build anticipation in the customer's mind and make them want to stick around for the grand finale. In short, it's about keeping your audience on the edge of their seats, so they're captivated to the very end.

So, here's what I did:

1 – I started by saying no.

2 – She asked me to reconsider. The ball was in my court.

3 – I told her that I sometimes make exceptions for a few special entrepreneurs.

4 – I followed up with an email a few days later, saying that I had given it some thought, and that I would send her an offer the next day.

5 – She wrote back, saying that she was eager to receive my proposal.

6 – I sent it to her the next day, as planned, giving her three options to choose from, and scheduled a phone call to discuss it further.

The result: I received her bank transfer the next day even before we spoke, despite the fact that it was much more expensive than she'd expected.

Curiosity and anticipation are generally winning strategies for building people's interest over time.

In his article published in *The Atlantic*, "Buy Experiences, Not Things," James Hamblin says that the more time we spend looking forward to an experience or a thing, the more satisfaction we will get from it.

In other words, making yourself desirable has a direct impact on how happy your customers will be with your products or services.

Entrepreneurs generally use this technique when they:

Make VIP offers

Launch new products

Publish content

Attract new talent

Launch their new brand image

Steve Jobs, Apple's former CEO, was a champion at this. Every time he launched a new product, he would leak just enough information about it for rumors to spread. Then, at the very end of his presentations, he'd unveil the next big thing by saying, "One more thing…." It drove Apple fans absolutely wild.

Practice revealing just enough, at just the right time. Follow a logical order, to create just the right amount of excitement.

Become a striptease champion.

HOW TO BREAK UP WITH YOUR PAST EVERY WEEK

Meeting new people is an essential part of growth, both for entrepreneurs and their growing businesses.

In addition to business development, it has another important purpose: It helps you cut ties and forge your own path. Remember, "No prophet is accepted in his hometown" (Luke 4:24).

Once, during a family meal, my sister and sister-in-law told me about some entrepreneurs they knew who thought they were lucky to be related to me because of my influence as an entrepreneur-consultant.

Their response: "Meh...."

I get the same reaction from people I worked with back at the beginning of my career, and you probably face the same awkward situation with some of the people you know.

Most of the people you've known for a long time will probably always see you as that person they met years and years ago, despite all the knowledge and experience you've gained since then. Your parents will always see you as their baby. The same goes for your former schoolmates, friends, ex-bosses and colleagues, your first clients, suppliers and partners, and members of your family.

You have to expand your network of contacts to include people who haven't known you very long, to avoid being trapped by your past.

I've been doing it for years, even when I really don't feel like it. I force myself to grow my network by taking the time to reach out in a meaningful way to at least two new people every week.

Always pick people who could potentially bring in business or become clients, or turn out to be someone you can recommend to others down the road.

Schedule a call, a coffee, a meal, or a company visit. Take the time to get to know each other and share your goals, to find out if you're a good fit on a personal and professional level.

I call this my +2 rule.

Adding two (+2) people every single week makes 100 more people getting to know you every year, starting today.

It's always easier to impress strangers than people who've known you for years There's tremendous growth potential in starting with an empty slate. It's one of the reasons why I don't particularly recommend networks with permanent members who meet on a regular basis.

Think about the sheer marketing potential of taking this step.

Don't get stuck in a rut by spending all your time with the same people.

BITING OFF MORE THAN I CAN CHEW AGAIN

Every year I fall into the same trap. I always eat too much when my family gets together for a meal. It might have something to do with accepting that third slice of carrot cake. In the moment, it's so good. A few hours later, not so much. I feel sick for the rest of the night, which makes me even grumpier than usual.

The exact same thing sometimes happens as we grow our businesses.

However focused we may be on the success of our business endeavours, we still try to take a bite out of every other opportunity that presents itself.

We sponsor everything.

We enter into every kind of partnership.

We accept all meeting requests.

We attend every networking or training event.

We treat all our customers like royalty.

We buy products and services we don't really need.

The list goes on…

If you don't learn to say no early on, you'll be choked by your own enthusiasm and gluttony.

Ask yourself this question: Do I need to seize this opportunity, given my current circumstances?

"I absolutely have to take this opportunity now, because it will never appear again."

Honestly.

An old traveling salesman once told me that he could sell anything to anyone by making them think it was a temporary opportunity. "You have until Friday to make your decision, but remember, it's a once-in-a-lifetime opportunity. If I don't hear from you, I'll be sharing this offer with your competitors…"

It could even be true, but the real question to keep in mind is whether it's a good strategic opportunity for you, or for the seller.

I also totally agree with Richard Branson, CEO of Virgin, whom I greatly admire. He says, "Business opportunities are like buses, there's always another one coming."

In business, you always have a choice, so make the most of it. If you don't, you'll be seen as an easy victim, and the old sharks will take advantage of your ignorance and your money.

IT'S YOUR FAULT

When I was working at BLV Transport, my biggest challenge was putting together a functional, independent team at a moment's notice. Why? Because no one was available to oversee the office employees full-time.

From the beginning, I ran into a lot of trouble with the project. Some of the challenges had to do with the management of human resources, specifically the recruitment, onboarding and supervision of employees.

Daniel Paré of Daniel Paré Auto was my mentor for nearly two years while I was at BLV Transport.

"Daniel," I asked him, "Why don't my employees do their jobs, so I don't have to fire them? I mean, it's not my fault they're incompetent."

"Alex, you're at least 50% responsible."

"Why?"

"Look in the mirror, Alex. Who hired them?

Yep, that stung.

That's why I tell entrepreneurs that it's their fault if they have problems with their employees.

Far too often, they don't make the job description, responsibilities and related tasks clear before starting the hiring process. They don't conduct formal interviews, check references from former employers, or verify potential employees' skills, and, worst of all, they don't evaluate their attitudes. I'm sure you've heard the saying "People are hired for their skills and fired for their attitude."

"Of course. But Alex, you can't evaluate people's attitudes."

Not true. In fact, there are countless personality tests available. Personally, I use MPO. It's an effective management program, and now that I've become a Creacor partner, I train business leaders in how to use it. I always ask my business partners and company employees, and even my clients, to take this type of personality test. It gives me a better understanding of the person and how to get the best results from them, and helps me make sure that the right people are in the right positions.

In my opinion, it's an absolute must if you want to boost your success as an entrepreneur and a leader.

So if you have a problem employee, whose fault is it?

"All right, but he never used to be like this. He's changed…"

Then why are you putting up with him?

WHAT DO YOU DO WITH A BAD APPLE?

To pick up where we left off in the previous chapter, I once let a toxic employee stay on at BLV Transport. She had the necessary skills, and she did her work well when she was in the mood. That said, she had a complicated personal life that had a negative effect on her performance and the energy of the entire group.

She was always coming in late for a thousand and one reasons beyond her control, she missed work far too often for family reasons, her relationship problems affected the atmosphere in the office, and she spoke disrespectfully to her manager.

I kept letting it slide because I absolutely needed her.

However, after several disciplinary warnings, meetings and second chances, I had no choice but to fire her. Some of my best employees were getting frustrated. They didn't understand why I was tolerating her questionable behaviour when they weren't given the same leeway.

The day after I let her go, one of my other employees came to see me and said it was about time; he'd gotten so fed up with the situation that he'd started looking for a job elsewhere.

We all know the old saying: one bad apple spoils the bunch.

I recently shared this anecdote with a client from one of my entrepreneurial coaching programs who was having trouble with one of his employees. He was stuck with an employee, a mechanic, who thought he was a superstar even though the quality of his work wasn't great. I told him that, despite the labour shortage, it was in his own best interest to let the employee go before he could do any more harm. He had no future in the business anyway.

One week later, the mechanic in question acted in a completely inappropriate manner towards a customer. The entrepreneur fired him on the spot, confiding in me later that he wouldn't have had the courage to do so prior to our discussion.

Remember that good employees attract more good employees, while bad employees only attract problems.

There's only one thing to do with a bad apple: throw it out.

LETHAL DISCOUNTS

Discounts or price reductions can provide the occasional boost to a business' sales. It's a technique that's been around for a very long time, and resale companies like Groupon and Tuango have used it to their advantage, often at the expense of participating entrepreneurs.

Whenever someone in my network tells me they want to offer a special discount to attract new customers, I reply by observing that they must not like their business since they seem to be trying to run it into the ground.

Offering discounts is suicidal. It's an appalling, perverse technique that can be lethal for several reasons.

To begin with, discounts tend to attract a particularly unsavoury type of customer that will only drain your energy and time without generating the profits you need to grow your business. You'll struggle in the short term, and you won't see any improvement in the long term because your stupid decision will force you to hire unskilled employees that you wouldn't otherwise need.

Also, discounts set a new point of reference for customers. Now they'll just wait until you announce the next discount to buy your products, and they won't know how much your services are actually worth anymore. This ultimately sinks your value. What makes it suicide? Because you chose to do it! Consider this: Who actually paid full price when they bought goods at the now-defunct Sears?

How many regular, paying customers have you gained by offering a steep discount?

I'm pretty sure I already know your answer.

Offer value instead of lowering your usual prices and rates.

How?

Offer a meaningful gift that isn't one of your usual products or services.

Create a fixed price chart based on volume of purchase.

Don't negotiate.

Develop one-of-a-kind services or special products unique to your company.

Offer exclusive products.

Charge a different price for pre-orders.

The list goes on...

But please, whatever you do, stop offering discounts to attract new customers.

IT'S ALWAYS MORE
OF THE SAME

If you only knew how many times I've used the concept of mental equivalence[6] to get an entrepreneur to charge more! It's mind-boggling.

Far too many entrepreneurs push themselves to the limit in an attempt to make some money, with nothing to show for it. They act more like a dog chasing its tail than reasonable people building successful businesses.

It's always the same old story: They don't charge their customers what their products or services are really worth.

I always start my presentations the same way. I draw their attention to the price difference between their business' products/services and those of their competitors.

They are almost always less expensive.

"Is it because the quality of your company's services

isn't as good as your competitors' services?"

"Not at all! We're much better, and our customers tell us so."

"Well then why do you charge less?"

"I don't know… My customers can't afford to pay more."

"Bullshit. Did they actually say that? If not, don't make assumptions."

When was your last price increase?

Your prices should go up every year. If you don't, you're leaving money on the table, and you'll have to keep playing catch-up because the cost of living is always increasing. You should at least be raising your prices at the same rate as inflation, which is between 2% and 3% annually, or at the same rate as your competition.

Does the price of gas, supplies, transportation, rent, insurance and employee salaries decrease or increase each year?

Let's face it: In general, the only customers who whine about price increases are the ones you don't really want to work with anyway. So, kill two birds with one stone. You'll make more money, and you'll get rid of customers who can't support your growth anyway.

Bingo! You win!

You'll perfect your current customer portfolio before you've even started attracting new customers. It's the most cost-effective investment you can possibly make.

So do it.

WE'RE NOT LIVING IN THE 80S ANYMORE

I had a brief exchange on social media with Philippe, one of the many pseudo-experts dishing out "expert advice" to entrepreneurs even though he's never owned a business or provided any kind of structured business development assistance before.

The bone of contention: the value of an entrepreneur's time.

He told a group of entrepreneurs that, instead of hiring additional resources, they should be putting in between 80 and 100 hours per week if they wanted to be successful because, in his opinion, "overtime put in by the entrepreneur is free."

In a private chat, I asked him where he got his information, but he only cited great entrepreneurs from a bygone era.

"It's not the 80s, 90s, 2000s, or even the early 2010s anymore. Working 80 hours a week is irresponsible."

I can tell you from experience that we stop being effective once we hit that threshold. We exhaust ourselves, which has a negative impact on our decision-making skills. Our mood is far from optimal, we start cutting corners and it becomes more and more likely that we'll just throw in the towel. Also, the financial results don't give us an accurate picture of what it costs to run the company, since we're doing the work of two people.

It's totally irresponsible. I don't know any rational person who would actually say that they do their best work under such circumstances.

Working 100 hours a week is a choice that leads only to unhappiness, frustration and, more often than not, the hospital.

Every entrepreneur I have coached who was working those kinds of hours when we started working together was on the brink of a breakdown. They confided in me that they no longer had a life, and felt guilty for not being around to see their children grow up. Others had suffered major health repercussions, which forced them to learn to work smarter. That doesn't necessarily mean working harder or longer hours, but working in a better way.

Going all in for a few weeks is one thing. But don't forget that burning the candle at both ends is never an effective long-term strategy.

If anyone ever tells you that you should work 100 hours a week over a long period of time because "your time costs nothing," run as fast as you can in the opposite direction.

Are you working too much?

"I'M REALLY BAD WITH NUMBERS"

I was chatting with an entrepreneur who offers marketing consulting services who confessed: "I should really take an accounting course, because I'm really bad with numbers."

"How exactly would that help you with your business?

People have a natural tendency to try and improve their weaknesses and shortcomings. If you want to stay right where you are, that's great. But it's counterproductive for those who want to make progress.

You can't be good, efficient and cost-effective at everything. So why are you trying so hard to turn yourself into a robot?

Your focus should always be on your strengths and developing your natural talents. We all have unique abilities that make us stand out. It's much more compelling to work on honing your skills in a field you are comfortable with and enjoy.

An entrepreneur's intelligence lies in their ability to surround themselves with people who are not only compatible but also more competent. Make up for your shortcomings by working with employees, partners and suppliers who are better at those things than you.

Tell me, is it more profitable to sweep the floor yourself, or to focus on customer acquisition and management?

Do you want growth, or stagnation?

BE GENEROUS

Some of you may call me out for getting a little sentimental here, but I have a confession to make.

In 2011, I attended a conference on business trends led by Michel Nadeau and Jevto Dedijer that had a huge influence on me as an entrepreneur-consultant. What really stuck with me was the concept of "random acts of kindness." For example, every day some businesses would randomly offer a $1 hotel room to one of their customers who booked online, and gave others free gifts. The companies did this without asking anything in return. Of course, word-of-mouth marketing was their ultimate goal.

Ever since that talk, I've gotten into the habit of doing something generous every month:

- Leaving a big tip for an employee expecting to receive $1.

- Providing a free consultation to entrepreneurs who really need it.

- Giving out a free copy of one of my books at random.

- Giving away any books I no longer need.

- Give away my shirts to someone else in my network (because I've worn them in too many photos).

- Giving an hourglass to someone who needs to be reminded that time is not a renewable resource.

- Paying for someone who's in a rush at the grocery store.

- The list goes on…

Many of the recipients ask me why I'm doing it.

It's just a way of giving back for all the success I've found doing what I love in life.

I think we all have a responsibility to be generous to others every now and then.

ARE YOU STUCK IN ANOTHER ERA?

I 've always been fascinated by history. Knowing where we come from allows us to build on the foundation of achievements, knowledge and theories that came before us, contributing to the continuous evolution of humanity.

The same goes for business. Understanding how capitalism has evolved to become what it is today is both compelling and enlightening.

Economic models in the business world have evolved at the same speed. The way we launch and manage companies now is very different from what it was 20 years ago, or even 10, 5, or just one year ago.

Entrepreneurship has become more accessible. New technologies that used to be available only to large companies are now within reach for almost anyone through annual subscriptions, and you don't need to own a complex, physical IT setup to use them.

So, what are you waiting for? Why not take advantage of these tools to pull yourself and your business out of the Stone Age?

- Did you know that your clients can book an appointment with you directly online, without confirming it with you first?
- Are you familiar with the wide range of communication tools and channels now available?
- Does it sound like I'm speaking Greek if I say Beenote, Slack, Drive, Trello, Zoho, ERP, Office 365, WooCommerce, Dropbox, Kiwili, Momenteo, Asana, Calendly, MailChimp, WordPress, or Wix?

Are you living on the same planet and in the same era as the rest of us?

OTHER THOUGHTS

Facebook groups for entrepreneurs
What do you value more: the opinions of a bunch of total strangers, or feedback from seasoned professionals, your own network, and your family?

Who are you going to actually listen to in this cacophony of voices? Helpful comments are often drowned out by nonsense from people who just make things up and repeat whatever they've heard someone else say.

So many people will give you advice even though they have no real understanding of your situation, and they don't care about the consequences.

Do it right the first time
Instead of slapping on a *Band-Aid* to temporarily hide a problem, then forgetting about it, do it right the first time. Fix it and move on.

Networking
What's the point of always networking in the same

place with the same people? ? If you do, don't come crying to me about not being able to find new customers or expand your contact network! You have to try new things if you want different results.

Punctuality

A late entrepreneur is more often than not a disorganized entrepreneur. Being late makes people wonder about your professionalism, skills and the quality of your work.

Unfortunately, some people seem to think that being on time is optional.

Diversify your sources

Too many entrepreneurs always get their information form the same places, rather than diversifying the source of their content. Instead, they should regularly seek out other authors, entrepreneurs, journalists, influencers, bloggers and specialists in fields related to what they do.

I'm always telling my clients to try other people's *Kool-Aid* too, not just mine. It's important to develop your own unique vision, not just copy others. Be critical at all times : blindly following others is what feeds the egos of certain so-called gurus.

Abundance creates independence

To me, abundance means having several excellent clients, strong sales, decent profits, outstanding employees, and exceptional partners. Together, these factors give you the power to be more selective about your contracts and negotiate from a strong position, because you don't have to grab every opportunity that presents itself.

In other words, you don't compromise just to keep your business afloat. You're not a slave to your clients and your business anymore. You have the freedom to choose.

Being in a position of abundance is what lets you develop your business with confidence.

Who doesn't want that?

Are you at the top of your game?

Are you in good physical shape?

Do you eat well?

Are you mentally energized?

Do you sleep well?

Do you learn something new every day?

Are you full of energy?

To be successful, you have to find the right balance for YOU, not whatever's being touted by other people or the society we live in.

Becoming the best possible version of yourself will give you confidence. Being confident makes it easier for others to trust you, which in turn accelerates the growth of your business.

Why not turn that to your advantage?

You know what you need to do.

So, what are you waiting for?

Luck is not a business strategy

Never leave your future to chance. Always take action. And decide what action to take based on the fact that your customers and your competition are also moving forward.

The first time

It's normal to feel proud when you succeed at something for the first time. But don't be presumptuous enough to think that you're now an expert at it. There's always room for improvement. And someone always pays the price for our first times.

LOOK IN THE MIRROR, KIDDO

During one of my training workshops, an entrepreneur told the group that his greatest concern was his younger employees' lack of motivation, criticizing everything they did.

"Young people these days just don't want to work. They're constantly asking for time off. They're lazy…"

Bla bla bla.

He went on and on for several minutes, with the thirty or so other participating entrepreneurs nodding their agreement, until I broke in with my trademark smirk:

"I think we all get the picture. Funny, I haven't run into this kind of situation at all, and I employ quite a few "young people" in one of my businesses. How do you expect your employees to respect you if you don't respect them?"

Your attitude towards your employees has a direct

impact on their performance and attitude towards you.

The key word here is respect.

Start by ignoring all the myths about different generations. They're nothing but oversimplifications of survey results. Who ever thought that Donald Trump would become President of the United States? How reliable are all those studies?

Stop assuming you know your employees' ambitions, skills and attitudes, and what motivates them. You're only seeing stereotypes based on your interactions with them. Get to know them, and ask them questions instead of guessing.

Help them grow with your company and work towards achieving their goals. Give them the training they need, and be generous. And if they leave your business to pursue their dreams instead of yours, that's fine.

They will be eternally grateful to you, and will become some of your best ambassadors.

Keep an open mind, and listen to them They have more to offer than you realize. Each of them has unique abilities, opinions and perspectives that are different from yours, and can be beneficial to your business.

And above all, be honest with them. They don't need to know the details of the company's financial situation, but make sure they see the connection between their own work and company performance.

EVERYONE MAKES MISTAKES

In my early twenties, I arrogantly told my father to his face that I'd never known failure and hadn't made any bad decisions so far in my life, adding that it was unlikely I'd ever make any.

That was before becoming an entrepreneur and experiencing entrepreneurial uncertainty.

I learned the meaning of the word *uncertainty* while I was working at BLV Transport.

BLV Transport was by far my best business school. I made countless mistakes and poor decisions, but I can assure you that my failures improved and accelerated my learning process.

The lessons I learned there cannot be taught in any classroom. I'd love to write more about everything that happened to me there, but legal entrepreneur and author Sylvie Bougie warned me not to in the strongest possible terms, for fear or of potential lawsuits. So I'll just let you imagine the stupid stunts I pulled.

We make our decisions based on our personalities and attitudes, and the knowledge, experience and information available to us in the moment.

Decisions made under those conditions are not always ideal or perfect.

That's what entrepreneurship is all about.

However, it's up to you, as an entrepreneur and manager, to limit the number of bad decisions and any impacts they may have.

How do you minimize risk?

The most important thing to do is to figure out what happened and keep it from happening again at all costs. Of course, you'd have to be a bull-headed idiot to keep repeating the same mistakes over and over again, expecting different results.

Do you take the time to learn from your mistakes, every single time you make one?

Learn, and be resilient.

WHAT ABOUT YOUR PARTNERS?

I'm frequently stern with entrepreneurs who have had the same partners ever since their businesses began. I always ask them this question:

"Are your partners still adding value?"

Our partners shouldn't be a burden that prevents us from moving in the right direction.

I once had a client who owned an auto repair shop. He used to complain that his partner, who was 10 years older than he was, was holding him back from pursuing his goals because he was focused on retirement, not on growing the business.

An entrepreneur in the health industry told me she was managing operations on her own, but was nonetheless forced to consult with her partners before making any decisions.

A factory owner was frustrated with his father's

extravagant personal use of company money, which was hurting the business's financial standing and growth prospects.

In my view, the value of a partner lies in the emotional, strategic or financial support they provide, based on the mission, vision and values of the business.

if they aren't providing that kind of support, you need to have at least one discussion with them to make some much-needed changes, or, in the worst-case scenario (which may be for the best), to negotiate a separation.

In any personal or professional circumstances, people come in and out of our lives as the situation develops. It's important to know how to cut ties when the time comes, to avoid creating conflict.

Are your partners necessary and strategic?

And an even bigger question: Are you, yourself, a good partner?

WHO IS YOUR SUBSTITUTE PLAYER?

I was in discussions with the executive director of an economic development organization in Central Québec about the possibility of hosting one of my group entrepreneurship programs in the region. "I love your coaching program, and your referrals from other regions of Québec are all excellent. But what if something happens to you midway through the contract and you aren't able to complete the program?"

"That's a great question, and I have to admit, it's something no one has ever asked me before. As you can imagine, the content and coaching techniques are designed to allow someone competent to take my place at the drop of a hat. Nicolas Roy or Michel Ross could easily replace me starting tomorrow morning. I teach my clients not to make themselves indispensable, and I'd be a pretty poor role model if I didn't apply my own advice, wouldn't I?

Just as I was writing these lines, my partner at Kérozn Communication, Josée Duchesne, gave me a call to check in following her vacation.

"I still don't know how I did it, but I somehow managed to fracture my right arm at the water park. Now I have to wear a brace, and since I'm right-handed, I can't really do any computer work."

Definitely not the best news for a busy graphic designer.

"I've spoken to Julie, and she'll be helping me out over the next month. She's been with us for over a year now, and does great work."

Wow, what a pleasant surprise: an entrepreneur with a plan to deal with this kind of unforeseen circumstance.

Injuries are seldom planned. But it's your responsibility to set up a fall-back plan to mitigate the consequences for you and your customers should an unforeseen event occur.

It's a matter of professionalism, and respect for your customers.

Throughout my career, I've watched customers desert companies whose owners ran into health issues that affected their ability to honour commitments and continue expanding their businesses.

No matter how much your clients value you, if you're unable to meet their needs they will take their business elsewhere. It's what always happens to businesses that depend entirely on their owners.

Is that what you want?

I FORGOT

"Sorry, I forgot to call you back."

"Oops, I forgot all about our appointment."

"I forgot to send you that report."

"I forgot to get back to you as promised."

This is an amateur response, and shows a negligence that borders on indifference.

There is no good reason not to follow through on your commitments, and even less of a reason to forget something.

"It's not a big deal."

It's true that, in most cases, no one will die because you forgot something. But it will affect your professional reputation.

Would you do business with someone who forgot their appointment with you?

Some people would argue that one mistake doesn't define us, and I agree. But please. We all have a handy tool in our pockets that puts our calendars within easy reach and lets us take notes so we don't forget anything.

Forgetting an appointment or urgent paperwork isn't like forgetting to buy milk at the store.

Your memory is far from infallible, and the more business you do, the more likely it is that your mind will play tricks on you.

Take notes constantly, even if you *never* forget things…

There's a first time for everything, and the first time something slips your mind can really cost you.

HOW TO SHOOT YOURSELF IN THE FOOT

The best way to lose control and become a slave to your business is to grow too fast and hire incompetent employees who don't match the profile you really need.

If only you knew the number of entrepreneurs who have told me they wished they could clone themselves...

In my opinion, that would be the worst mistake they could make.

Ask yourself this question: Would you be able to interact all day with an employee who was an exact replica of you?

I can tell you right away that I wouldn't want to work with another Alexandre Vézina.

And I'm convinced that it's not really what you want either, even if you think you'd be able to get more work done. It might work pretty well for a while, but eventually conflicts would arise.

What you really want is to build a company with employees with complementary skills who make up for your shortcomings, employees who are better than you are at their respective tasks.

Forgive me if I borrow an overused saying from my friends in human resources management:

We often hire people for their skills, and let them go for their attitude and toxic behaviour.

So I'd like to share two essential questions that you should always ask during the interview process before hiring a candidate:

1) What did you like most about your former bosses?

2) What could your former bosses have done better, or in what circumstances do you feel they should have acted differently?

It will give you a way to evaluate their personal values, and find out what they consider important in the workplace and their interactions with their supervisor.

As someone who has made too many mistakes in the past, I also ask every employee we hire to complete a personality test. It's a tool that we mainly use to make sure that the new employee is a good fit for the position for which they are being hired. It also helps us provide the support they need to do their job well, without judgment.

I believe that it's the employer's responsibility to ensure the well-being of the employees they hire by assigning them to a post that's right for them.

If not, take a deep breath and show them the door.

I HAVE 15 YEARS' EXPERIENCE

"**I**'ve owned my business for 15 years."

So what?

The number of years' experience a person has and the amount of time a company has existed mean nothing.

Numbers can say whatever we want them to. And above all, in my opinion, a year in the life of a risk-taking entrepreneur is much fuller than a year of just getting by for a lazy entrepreneur.

If you do the same things over and over again and make the same kinds of decisions week in, week out, never feeling like you're making progress, I don't see that as a valuable year of experience. You're nothing but a fish swimming in circles in a little pond.

It goes without saying that entrepreneurs are self-taught people who continually develop their knowledge and skills to meet their needs.

If this is true, you must first and foremost become a specialist in the field that provides your main source of income. You have to at least know more than your customers and Google about your area of business, and keep yourself well-informed of the latest developments in your field. If I can stump you on your own business and field of expertise after a quick Internet search, you've got a major problem. Back in the 80s, you could say just about anything to your customers and sound like God, just by reading the specs for the product you were selling. But those days are over.

Let me illustrate my point. I was recently talking to a sales specialist who claimed to be the best in his field, when he'd never even heard of Colleen Francis, Jeb Blount, Jeffrey Gitomer or John Jantsch. within the space of 10 seconds, he lost all credibility in my eyes. He was like a half-blind hermit on a deserted island, reminiscing about his former glories.

Read the books written by leaders in your field. It will nurture your creativity, support you in developing new concepts beyond theirs, and help make your clients more successful. You'll learn more, and compare yourself to the best. If you aren't doing this, you're just one entrepreneur among thousands, and the disappearance of your business will go unnoticed because it will never be more than a pale copy of the others.

You should also be seeking out new experiences on a regular basis, to get you out of your comfort zone, increase your self-confidence and develop your mental equivalence[7]. Basically, you need to make your true value stand out in comparison to the competition, so that your customers will be ready to pay fairly for the value you have to offer.

Finally, find inspiration in what is happening in the world and in fields other than yours. Use it to incorporate new ideas into your business and stay ahead of the competition. When you are well-informed, it elevates you in the eyes of others, especially in our age of disposable information where people so often discuss things superficially without any understanding of the nuances, and with no ability to sustain a real conversation.

Don't try and tell me that you don't have time, when it's probably one of the only ways to keep from being overwhelmed and bringing your business down with you. Those who do take the time will pass you by and leave you in the dust.

If you don't have time to stay competitive and make a real difference in your customers' lives, shut your business down now and find a job someplace else. I know a lot of entrepreneurs looking for qualified employees right now...

"ALEX, YOU'VE BEEN HAD!"

Early in my career, I ran into a young serial entrepreneur named Samuel several times. At that point in my career, we had similar views on business. I have to admit that my initial goal was to buy his media company and make it part of my other businesses managed by Gestion Watson. At that point, it was a valid strategy that would have accelerated the time to market of my future entrepreneurial acquisitions.

During one discussion, I told him about the subtleties of my business model as a first-time entrepreneur-consultant, and my recipe for success.

After playing around with a few different directions for his company, he ended up letting it slide. We lost touch.

Some time later, he gave me a call.

He told me that he'd started helping companies position themselves on the Web to increase their numbers of leads and close deals with added value.

"Good for you, Samuel."

"I've analyzed your website, and I can help you convert more customers by buying several keywords that represent you. I'll email you."

"You know me well enough to know that I don't use that kind of approach for my work."

"Just take a look, Alex. If you're still not interested, I can sell the exact same package to one of your competitors."

A few months later, an entrepreneurial training organization in Québec City started presenting their services by using exactly the same language I use for mine. They were even shameless enough to use the term "entrepreneur-consultant" for their group of experts.

I have to admit, it really annoyed me... for about 15 minutes. There are so many entrepreneurs and pseudo-experts who do nothing but copy other people. Copying is a strategy used by amateurs who are always one step behind.

Have you ever noticed that certain unscrupulous people will try to make money off of your expertise and your network of contacts?

It's a threat to your business.

When I talked to my partner, Nicolas Roy of Gestion Watson, about it, he laughed, saying, "Alex, you've been had again!"

Nicolas was reminding me that this wasn't the first time I'd shared too many details about my business with entrepreneurs whose companies I wanted to buy. He'd seen me place my trust in people too quickly before, mainly by granting them access to certain prestigious members of my business network, an access they were all too quick to take advantage of.

After paying a steep price for my generosity, to the point of damaging my business relationship with one of my long-standing contacts, I told myself that I absolutely had to be more careful about making recommendations and revealing strategic aspects of my business.

Now, I start by taking the time to meet the individual or the owner of the company several times, and talking about a variety of general subjects It gives me the opportunity to see whether their values and mine are in alignment by talking face to face.

Then I check to make sure we have the same business philosophy.

I contact members of my network who have already worked with them for references.

As soon as I notice anything that doesn't mesh, I put the brakes on the process and move on. Whenever possible, I test the quality of the products or services myself before referring the business to someone else, or sharing my upcoming entrepreneurial projects.

I look for quality partners that I can rely on and truly trust.

Isn't that what you want too?

STEALING IS
NOW A MUST

I've been to my local hardware store several times recently because I'm building a new patio[8]. Every time I go, the same employee greets me with a smile and a friendly "hello." Once I overheard her making calls to customers and taking orders in a very professional manner. She was only about 20 years old.

If I owned a retail business in or near Pont-Rouge, I definitely would have offered her a job with my company. Yes, I would happily "steal" this employee from another store owner.

Almost all of my clients are in the process of growing their businesses. The biggest challenge they face is finding qualified people to hire who fit the company's culture and the direction of its growth. Yet they are reluctant to recruit good employees from other companies.

"Oh, I couldn't do that. I wouldn't like it if someone

stole employees from me. Besides, it would damage my reputation."

All right…

So I ask them this question: Do you know what it's called when you choose not to hire excellent employees from other companies in the region?

<u>Self-sabotage.</u>

Most good employees won't be unemployed when you need them, and they won't usually be actively trying to change jobs. But you can try to draw their interest or attract their attention.

Let's make one thing clear right away: employees are not the property of the business they work for. They are individuals who are paid to do the job that has been given to them. More importantly, they are human beings, capable of making their own decisions when an opportunity appears to make a change for the better.

No matter what, the decision to accept a new job or not is entirely up to the employee. If they're happy with their current job, they won't consider your offer. But the seed you planted in their mind will remain, and whenever they have an annoying experience with their employer, they will think of you.

Guess what could happen next.

They'll call you back a few months later, and you'll gain a fantastic employee.

Are you nervous about doing it yourself? Are you just too busy? Then I recommend using a recruitment firm.

They'll do it for you, for a commission. Isn't finding competent, independent, reliable employees worth the investment?

Stop waiting for people to send you their resumes; that's just not how it works anymore.

And don't be naive enough to think that your competitors aren't out there trying their luck. They may already be signing on with recruiting firms, and guess which company's employees they'll target first...

DO YOU REALLY KNOW YOUR CLIENTS?

It always amazes me when my clients don't really know their own clients.

In general, people do business with people they like and who show genuine interest in them. You're lucky enough not to be a multinational corporation whose clients are nothing but a series of numbered folders. You can offer a strong argument that distinguishes you from those corporations: proximity.

Give me the name of one of your clients, and within five minutes I'll know almost as much about them as you do.

The Internet and social media are full of people's personal information, including their travel photos, vacations, children, animals, goals, and more. Take advantage of this tool before you talk with any of your customers or prospects.

It's a way of showing interest in who they are, and their lives outside the workplace. And don't tell me that you don't have time to get to know your clients, because that would definitely earn you a smack from a two-by-four!

Every time you find common interests with one of your clients, you create a closer bond and a stronger business relationship. You can find something in common with almost anyone if you look hard enough. There's art, music, sports, politics, home renovations, cars, TV shows, hobbies, or even Chuck Norris.

Let's get real: your best clients are what move your business forward. So take good care of them. Call them **at least** twice a year just to chat about what's new in their lives, without any ulterior motive. Your conversation will often end with your client making a purchase request, just because you showed a little interest in them!

How can you develop close relationships that transcend your business transactions, building your clients' commitment and loyalty, if you aren't interested in them?

ARE YOU PROUD OF THE QUALITY MEMBERS IN YOUR NETWORK?

Early on in my career as an entrepreneur, I had quality issues with suppliers in the transportation field. Let's just say that several of them had checkered pasts, and the others weren't particularly recommendable or trustworthy.

At the time, I promised myself that I would clean up my network of contacts and clients regularly, and would only maintain close business ties with people I would be happy to introduce to my spouse and children.

I take the same approach to recommending people or companies to my clients, or to any entrepreneurs who ask. I've been duped a few times, and I don't want it to ever happen again.

It's not the number of contacts in your network that's important, it's the quality of the individuals. Having 5,000 contacts on LinkedIn sounds cool. But the truth is, it's nothing but a charade and a way to boost our egos.

In general, we can maintain close relationships with about 125 people annually. When you have an effective network, each of those 125 people should be able to recommend at least one new potential client per year, **if you ask them to**.

Make your calculations based on the annual value of a new client for your business, and the conversion rate of the qualified leads provided by your network.

Imagine that the members of your network have given you 125 new potential clients. If the average value of one of your contracts is $1,000, and your average conversion rate is 25% (which is theoretically low for someone you've been introduced to by a mutual connection). This gives us the following formula: 125 x 1,000 x 25% = $31,250.

Be aware of the potential commercial value of every reference from your network, and track the performance of each. It will give you a clear picture of the strength of your network, and how valuable it is to you aside from the expertise of its members.

In my opinion, the true value of an individual or a company is shown by the quality of its relationships.

I am extremely proud of my network, and I hope you feel the same about yours.

If not, you know what you have to do. Eliminate

low value relationships immediately, because the reputations of the people you associate with will rub off on yours. Then, start building strong ties with people who are on your same wavelength.

YOUR JOB IS AT STAKE

D o you realize that your job as an entrepreneur is constantly at stake?

Or at least it should be.

Some of you will say that the business world is always risky. True, but that's not what I'm talking about.

Like so many others, Martin, a client of mine in the auto industry, was complaining one day about the salary he was paying himself.

"Martin," I interrupted, "if you were my employee or partner and you were complaining like this, looking at your salary in light of your business' performance, I'd get rid of you. Your work isn't worth half of what you pay yourself. You're too expensive compared to what you contribute. You're holding back the growth of your business."

Another of my clients, Isabelle, went in every day

to give instructions to her employees, going right over the heads of the managers she had hired to handle the operations and management of her business.

"Isabelle, do you realize that you're confusing your employees? You may be the boss, but that doesn't make it okay to undermine the authority of your managers."

My list of examples of this kind of behaviour goes on and on.

Whenever these situations arise, I explain to my clients that whenever I find myself getting too comfortable, I ask myself the following questions:

- Would I be willing to pay this salary to a stranger who had my attitude and skills and acted this way?
- Is my performance equal to the effort I put in?
- Would my employer be happy with my overall performance in terms of my responsibilities?
- Would I get rid of an employee who acted like this?
- Would I demand more from them?
- What kinds of improvements would I require them to make?

I recommend writing a job description for your position, including all of the accompanying tasks and responsibilities. Set goals for yourself, and set out any performance-related rewards (bonuses) or consequences in advance.

Every year, I reward myself if I reach my goals. For example, I bought myself a Mercedes when I signed my first major contract as a consultant, but when BLV Transport was shut down I got nothing.

Let's celebrate our good moves, learn from our failures and avoid getting complacent.

GO THE EXTRA MILE

There was a period of time last year when I got a little lazy, instead of putting in extra effort at one of my companies that needed it. I probably would have fired myself for my weak performance.

This sudden thought, inspired by the big question in the last chapter, forced me to whip myself into shape.

Every day, as soon as I'd "finished work," I forced myself to do one final thing that I normally would have put off until the next day.

- Call a client
- Send an email
- Prepare an invoice for a client
- Prepare an order
- Write down a procedure
- Check in with an employee
- Analyze the company's numbers
- Speak with a customer or employee

- Balance a cash register
- Write a blog post
- Post on social media
- Get in touch with a member of my network
- Stock the shelves
- Perform a quality test in the factory
- Listen to the voicemail messages
- Send a request to a supplier
- The list goes on...

Even if you're already working a lot, imagine what would happen if you could get just one more thing done every day, something that takes less than five minutes. By the end of the year, you would have accumulated 20 more hours of productive time by barely lifting a finger.

If that doesn't work for you, try starting your day just a little earlier. It's amazing how much we can get done before our employees, clients and partners start interrupting us.

Come on, don't be lazy! Take a second to go the extra mile before officially ending your day's work.

WHAT WILL PEOPLE THINK?

I went to the grocery store before giving a workshop in the greater Québec City area. Since my hands were full, I opened the trunk of my car before I got there. At the same time, a man drove up and parked next to my vehicle. He looked around but didn't see me coming, and stayed near my car.

We had the following conversation when I arrived:

"I thought it was strange that someone had left the trunk of their car open. I wanted to make sure no one would come along and steal anything. I have a friend who has a car like yours, and I'd like to have one too someday.

You're doing pretty well! You have a great car which, I have to admit, is worth more than mine.

Yeah, I have ten like this one."

"What? You own ten luxury cars and you can't get yourself a Mercedes?" I don't get it, you could probably buy dozens of these…"

"I'm the owner of a major funeral home. I have to drive this kind of vehicle. If I drove a car like yours, my customers would think I'm making too much money because of the image that comes with having a Mercedes. I'll get one when I retire."

The entrepreneur in question was at least 75 years old! He was keeping himself from having the car he truly wanted because of what other people might think. Wow…

Most of us put way too much importance on the judgments of others. It's only natural. We are social beings who want to be part of a community, a reference group. We don't want to be outcasts living on the outskirts of society. That means that we instinctively do things to please others as much as possible.

But we can't please everyone. In business, it's best to start by being respected before trying to be liked.

"What will people think?"

If you spend your life worrying about other people's opinions, you'll always be a sheep. If you let your individuality be your guide and refuse to be like everybody else, you'll be seen as a predator.

Which do you prefer?

I'm sure you already know my answer to that question, and how I feel it applies to entrepreneurship.

SPARE US THE SOB STORY

I referred a client with a unique, high-potential product to several members of my network, to help her accelerate the growth of her business and obtain financing from a private investor.

She started each meeting by talking about all the difficulties she had encountered in her private life, from childhood to adulthood, placing the blame on the people around her. She talked about herself and her loved ones the entire time.

Theoretically, a conversation is a two-way street.

The instability of her personal life, and her eagerness to talk about her business motivations without asking others about theirs, made her seem self-centred, although I can assure you that she isn't.

She made the mistake of laying all her cards on the table too soon, before she'd had time to build a relationship of trust with potential private investors.

My contacts were taken aback by her attitude, and one of them said,

"Alex, it's like she's desperate! It's as if she's cut her veins open and is spewing blood everywhere, clinging to me for dear life. Next time, make sure she's ready to act like a normal person before sending her someplace."

If you're desperate and acting like a chicken with its head cut off, I will let you run around until you fall down on your own and don't get up.

If you're going to indirectly damage my reputation, I don't want to get my hands dirty.

Is that clear?

Be polite and respectful when someone has given you a special introduction to their contacts in order to help you expand your business.

WHAT DO YOU LIKE TO DO?

At one of my weekly live sessions, Valerie, a client at the CAEQ, said: "Alex, I'm paralyzed by everything I have to do. I can't see things clearly anymore, and I'm exhausted."

"When you're not working on your business, what do you really love to do?"

"Take walks by the river while listening to music."

"Perfect. Take the afternoon off and go do that. Have a good day."

"But I have to work."

"I said, have a good day. In the state you're in, you wouldn't be able to get much done, you'd just go around in circles. Go get some fresh air."

I often tell entrepreneurs who are overworked or unfocused to take a half-day off to do something else.

It allows them to disconnect from the business for a little while and get their minds back on track.

For myself, I like to read, take a nap, play the guitar, take a walk, watch a movie or play Legos with my son.

The point is, pushing ourselves when we're not at our best isn't usually worth it, and it can often lead to insomnia.

I always tell my entrepreneur clients to take a three-day weekend at least once a month, to fully disconnect and recharge. There's a reason why there are so many federal holidays in the year.

When I started out, I kept working even when I was totally exhausted, and I wasn't very productive at all during those times. What was the point?

What do you do to clear your mind?

"I CAN'T DO THAT"

"**C**hristine, you absolutely have to increase your rates."

"Daniel, fire that employee immediately."

"Jade, focus on sales with the advisors."

"Julie, stop procrastinating and post this year's event calendar."

"Nancy, change financial institutions."

"Olivier, buy a new tractor."

"Emile, change your company name."

"Eve, get your new website online."

"Karl, make an offer to this potential employee."

"Patrick, sell 10% of your shares to that employee."

"Alex, I can't do that."

I understand that they're taken out of context, but all of my conversations generally end with advice and a mandatory action to take. Otherwise, we're just spinning our wheels instead of making progress.

Far too many experts ask questions without knowing the answers, and yet entrepreneurs need answers when they're not sure what to do next. They don't want to be asked a ton of questions by so-called business coaches in hopes that an answer will "emerge" from their subconscious.

"You asked me to answer your question because you're stuck and you value my opinion. That's what I did. I gave you the best possible solution for your situation. I'm not going to explain the whole intellectual journey I took to reach this conclusion, listing all the other options I considered that would be much less effective. I'd certainly do it if I was billing you by the hour for this advice. But that so-called "professional" practice is unethical, in my opinion, because some advisers stretch their explanations out so they can rake in more money[9]. Do you realize that you're the one who's limiting the growth of your business?"

Whenever you feel like saying "I can't do that," change your perspective and ask yourself how you can make it happen instead. What conditions could you set up that would make it possible?

I'd like to add a little clarification about the hourly billing model. If you're an entrepreneur who wants to be successful, avoid it at all costs.

Why? It's very simple.

A company that's always having to charge more hours forces its owner to work longer and longer to make more money. If you're stuck in this pattern, get out of it now.

By the way, passive income is an alternative, but it's not the only possibility, and for it to work well you have to start by setting a few other things up... But I can't give away all my secrets in my books!

Let's move on.

WE'RE 80% READY

During a meeting, Julie and Mireille of Yogami told me that they had a lot of potential new ideas, but were waiting for the perfect moment to launch them.

"If you're 80% ready, just do it. Be agile, don't let your perfectionism stop you. Most of your customers don't expect everything to be perfect. They want things to work, and they want to get value for money. The extra effort to make everything that much better isn't worth it if the client can't even tell. Let your actions accelerate your forward momentum."

What's the point of doing an impeccable job if no one notices the extra quality and the customer isn't ready to pay more for it?

Quality is a waste of time in these conditions.

The way I see it, a project that takes too long to complete with no significant gain in value, because its initiator is a perfectionist, is called a work of art.

The entrepreneurial cemetery is full of them.

Do you want your name to be engraved on an entrepreneurial tombstone too?

Be agile, be fast, and avoid falling into the trap of inertia that digs so many entrepreneurial graves. BLV Transport failed, in part, because of that law, and I wouldn't wish it upon anyone.

"An object at rest will remain at rest, while an object in motion will remain in motion at the same speed and in the same direction unless acted upon by an outside force."

In other words, an object (a person, situation, behaviour, etc.) will naturally tend to keep doing what it's already doing, unless something external happens that forces it to change.

Like a solid whack from a two-by-four.

Accelerated momentum is a key element.

The faster you move, the harder it is to stop you. And it's much harder to start moving when you're at a standstill, isn't it?

Remember your last vacation. When a break lasts too long, getting back to work again and finding our natural rhythm can be a real challenge.

Leave everyone else in the dust by staying active at all times.

EDUCATE THE MUGGLES

"In J. K. Rowling's Harry Potter series, a muggle is a person who lacks any sort of magical ability and was not born in a magical family."[10]

As far as I'm concerned, in our world, *muggles* are people who are unfamiliar with entrepreneurship.

I feel that every entrepreneur has a responsibility to educate these people when appropriate. Make them aware of what it really means to be an entrepreneur, and everything that goes with it: the risk, the stress, the long hours worked, the unusual schedules, etc.

Sometimes muggles are jealous when they see how successful you've been, but they don't necessarily realize how many sacrifices and concessions you've been making for years, or even decades for some entrepreneurs.

I sometimes let loose when a friend or an acquaintance

comments on my lifestyle, or sees my car in the driveway at 10 a.m. on a Friday. I ask them ,

- "Were you up this morning at 5 a.m. sending invoices to your clients?"

- "Did you spend last weekend working?"

- "Did you get off work at 11 p.m. yesterday?"

- "Have you ever had to take out a second mortgage on your house because of financial difficulties at your company?"

- "Did you pay your employees out of your own pocket last week?"

- "Would you be willing to work without pay for two years?"

- "Have you ever had insomnia because you don't know how to handle an issue with an employee?"

- "When you're supposedly spending time with your family, are you distracted because your brain is spinning at 100 miles an hour, trying to solve a business problem?"

- "Have you ever had to find a replacement for one of your employees on a Sunday night?"

- "Do you have to call clients back while you're watching your son's hockey game?"

- "Do you have 101 bosses?"

- "Do you have to go to work even when you're sick?"

- "Would you wait five years before taking a full week's vacation?"

- "Have you ever had only $18.00 in your bank account, so you couldn't get money out of the ATM?"

- "Do you have to work on holidays while your employees are enjoying time with their families?"

- "Do you think about your clients while you're doing the dishes?"

- "Do you live in constant fear of losing your best employee?"

- "Do you break out in hives every time they increase the minimum wage, because all your employees who make more than that will expect a raise too?"

- "Are you constantly adding items to your to-do list, even while you're sleeping?"

- "Do you feel guilty whenever you sit down in the living room with your family, because you still have 50,000 things you need to get done that day?"

- "Has your employer ever forgotten to pay you, and did you have to remind him over and over?"

- "Do you have to wait 90 days to get paid for your work?"

- "Have you ever had to prepare a major proposal at 8:45 p.m.?"

- "Do you live below the poverty line according to the official government measure because you have to reinvest all the money generated by your company?"

- "Have you had to empty your RRSPs to reinvest the money in your business, because no financial institution was willing to give you a loan?"

- "When you say that you'll be home around 6 p.m., does it end up being more like 7 p.m. because there was an emergency at work?"

- "Has your debt reached a theoretically impossible level?"

- "Do you have to engage in financial gymnastics to make ends meet at the end of the month, or to pay your taxes?"

- "Do you have to pay employees to do nothing to keep them from looking for a job elsewhere?"

I don't say these things to make them feel sorry for us. I just want them to realize that they're only seeing the tip of the iceberg, and that they have no idea what's really going on beneath the surface.

DO YOU NEED TO GET MOTIVATED?

Once, in a meeting with lawyer and entrepreneur Sylvie Bougie, she said: "Alex, I've spent two years telling myself that I want to grow my business, and that I need to find someone to help me."

"Why didn't you do it sooner?"

"That's easy. I was comfortable, and it was easier to just put the project off."

"What's changed? Why now?"

"I'm moving next month, and my new office has double the space. I have to expand."

Some entrepreneurs need someone to give them a good whack to get them to act, while others are able to give it to themselves.

Many of my clients invest in new equipment or new offices, hire new resources, buy a new business, and look for help afterwards.

It's what I call growth motivation.

They are forced to make their decision profitable by expanding their business. It throws their balance off temporarily, so that they have to move forward and strive to reach new heights.

One of my clients was getting sick of hearing me tell him to increase his rates at the end of each of our meetings. Then suddenly, one day, he announced that he'd raised them by 25%, putting his prices on par with the competition.

I was stunned. "Good, I said. "What's changed since our last meeting?"

"I have to pay for my new pickup truck."

You don't have to take that kind of step to grow your business. However, it is true that big decisions tend to force us out of our comfort zone and propel us to the next level.

What will it take to get you to act?

CAN YOU REALLY MOTIVATE YOUR EMPLOYEES?

The short answer: No.

Motivation is what drives us to act. Motivation is intrinsic. In other words, it's up to each of us to know ourselves, and to do things that motivate us regularly.

In the previous chapter, we saw that some people are motivated by progress and achieving their goals, while others may be motivated by things like

freedom, independence, challenges, progress, recognition for the achievement of goals, learning, project completion, self-expression, organization, structure, finding solutions, managing time, working with others or alone, concentration, variety, public appreciation, leadership, visibility, influence, accuracy, consistency, finishing one thing before starting another, harmony, competition, stability, recognition and attention, a sense of belonging to a group, independent thinking, being appreciated for their skills, being the one responsible, material proof that their work is appreciated, etc.

So it's up to each of us to know ourselves and to do things in our lives that we appreciate and that spark our enthusiasm.

When you do something you love, you don't need someone else to motivate you or offer you bonuses and rewards. It's nice to get them, of course, but is that really what motivates someone to do a good job?

If an employee always needs a wage incentive to be productive, they'll jump at the first opportunity to make more money elsewhere, because they'll never stop wanting more. Significant wage increases only have a temporary effect on a person's productivity and mood. So money isn't a sustainable source of motivation, because it only motivates people partially.

Anyway, let me assure you that you don't want that kind of individual working for your company. They're the ones who get grouchy every six months because they aren't paid enough for what they do. From their point of view, of course.

When I started out as an entrepreneur, I thought that money was my main source of motivation. All my investments were based solely on that one perspective, until I made my worst financial decision ever: investing my time and money in a company that didn't interest me. There were no advantages; the entire entrepreneurial endeavour was nothing but a burden from start to finish. It ended up draining my RRSPs and my investments, and temporarily distracting me from my other financial goals.

That was when I realized that what really motivated me was something else, and that money was only a result of making good deals.

To get back to what I was saying, what you want more than anything else are employees who enjoy their jobs and are paid fairly to do them. Period.

What you can do is make sure that you have the right conditions in place to bolster your employees' motivation.

Here's how:

1) Make sure that each of your employees is a good fit for their job (the right attitude, behaviour, needs, etc.).

2) Give them all the tools they need to do their job well.

3) Eliminate any major obstacles or irritants related to their position.

4) Help them understand the importance of their role in the company.

5)   Treat them with respect and being honest with them at all times.

6) Recognize the contribution they make to the company.

7) Provide them with training in areas they enjoy (related
to their work).

8) Help them to continually improve.

9) And above all, be considerate.

When it comes to your employees, being considerate means taking the time every day for a brief, sincere chat about their lives (activities, passions, hobbies, family, etc.).

I recommend the "One Minute"[11] technique.

Take one minute every day to talk to each of the employees you manage about something that interests them. It will help you develop a relationship with them, a stronger bond than the one that only exists because you pay them for their work. They're likely to be more loyal to the company if they feel appreciated and respected, rather than feeling like lemons being squeezed to the last drop.

Right?

If you have more than 20 employees, make sure your managers are doing the same thing.

WHAT MUSIC HAS TAUGHT ME

I started strumming the guitar at age 12. I have to admit, I was never what you'd call naturally talented at it.

After a few years of classes with Kathleen Arial, my guitar teacher at the time, she gave me the following gift:

"Alex, I have nothing more to teach you. It's time for you to stand on your own two feet. You have all the tools you need, and there's only one way to keep improving: Practice rigorously, and be disciplined about it."

From that moment on, I gradually stopped playing *for fun* and started playing to get better. At one point, I was playing up to 4 hours a day: 3 hours of electric guitar, 45 minutes of acoustic guitar and 15 minutes of bass. Also, a major guitarist had recommended that I replace all the strings on my instruments with larger ones to build up the calluses on my fingers faster. It made playing very uncomfortable, and after practicing for several hours my fingers often hurt. It was unpleasant and painful, but I was making faster progress, which was extremely rewarding.

It was easy for me to play almost anything, because I knew the vast majority of techniques used in contemporary songs. I could learn a song quickly with very little practice. I invested in several high-quality instruments, until at one point I owned twelve of them.

Music taught me that, by putting in the effort, studying with the best in the field (Steve Vai, Joe Satriani, John 5, etc.) and finding the right ways to accelerate the learning process, I could do just about anything.

Later, I transferred this approach to my entrepreneurial career by creating accelerated learning labs, owning businesses, investing, serving on boards of directors, and, most importantly, training other entrepreneurs.

Being an entrepreneur is like learning to play a musical instrument.

You start out by choosing a musical instrument that you feel drawn to, you buy it, and you try to play it on your own. You have fun playing simple songs that impress the people around you who don't know how to play.

Then comes the moment when you say, that's enough of that. You know that it's time to get out of your comfort zone if you want to progress to a whole new level.

So you invest in yourself to build your knowledge

and skills, but more than that, you start developing the strong sense of discipline you need to keep going.

You have to practice, practice, practice until your actions and decisions become reflexes that require less effort.

The discipline we learn by practicing lets us accelerate the pace of everything we do, and it becomes easy and natural for us to do so.

In short, you have to practice everything you want to improve in your business.

At one of my book launches, the wife of one of my clients pulled me aside to ask my advice.

"I dream of writing a book someday. What should I do?

"That's easy. Write. Take 15 minutes every day and write. One day, you'll move up to 30 minutes, and then even longer.

Every time you hit a plateau, in other words, every time you feel like you're stagnating, find yourself a mentor that can help get you over the hump. And please, make sure you find someone who has done it before. Avoid people who just ask you questions that even they don't know how to answer."

It's the simplest thing in the world: The more you practice, the more you work at it, the better you get.

And that's true of everything you do.

THE NOT-TO-
DO LIST

Melissa is the owner of a service company. She asked me what my secret is to being so effective in my various projects and my writing.

Alex, you're so annoying[12]. You never seem overwhelmed, and you always have time to get back to your clients. How do you do it?

It's easy: Stop wasting time on pointless things, like social media. Also, you have to know exactly what you need to do to achieve what you want to achieve, and most importantly, you have to know exactly what you should not be doing.

That's it. It's just a question of priorities. Stop complaining that you have too much to do. Having multiple priorities means only one thing: You've lost control and you have no priorities at all. You don't know what's important to you.

To keep improving as an entrepreneur and stop

complaining about a lack of time, I recommend using the concept of the *not-to-do* list. Basically, it's a list of things to avoid or to simply stop doing.

The first thing to decide on is what you want to accomplish. Without a destination, it's hard to choose the right path.

Then list everything that distracts you from your goals and isn't ideal based on your personality.

What do I have to stop doing to be more successful?

<u>Situations to avoid:</u> There are several kinds of situations in which you aren't at your best. For example, an introvert won't get great results at a happy hour event. There are so many other ways to grow your business these days.

<u>Behaviour to stop:</u> We all act in ways that don't further our goals from time to time. What kind of things do you do that sabotage your progress?

<u>Tasks to delegate:</u> You aren't good at everything, so you need help from others to avoid getting overwhelmed.

<u>Clients, suppliers, and contacts to avoid:</u> Some people are like vampires. They sap your energy, and you just don't feel good around them. Avoid them as much as possible.

The idea is to gain clarity by eliminating everything that is not essential to your success. That's why you should let go of at least 15% of your clientele every year. Increase your prices constantly. Regularly eliminate some of the products or services you offer. Pare down your network of contacts, and any current opportunities and projects.

Only perform tasks that are in alignment with your goals, and invest your company's resources in the kind of value creation that clients are willing to pay for.

YOU HAVE A CHOICE TO MAKE: BE LAZY, OR EVOLVE

When Jerry was struggling to expand his business in the field of technology, he asked me this question: "Alex, do you think I'm lazy?"

"Yes."

"Wow, okay. That's a pretty clear answer."

"Listen Jerry, if you're not ready to hear the answer, don't ask the question."

Far too often, we ask questions because we expect to hear something positive and precise. If that's what you want, find yourself a *Yes Man*[13] who will pay you pretty compliments and keep you from making progress. *Yes*

Men are usually people who lack self-confidence and want to please as many people as possible. They generally cost less but they're terrible advisors.

Progress hurts. Growth hurts. Shedding your old skin hurts.

Many animals, including snakes and lobsters, shed their skin. They get rid of their old skin or shell so they can grow better. As an entrepreneur, you should be doing exactly the same thing to help you evolve.

Evolving is not easy. It means coming face to face with yourself. It means changing categories. It makes the world bigger and more dangerous.

"I'm definitely not hiring you to be *nice* to me. Your point of view is valuable to me, Alex. Would you please explain?

"You've set up a customer attraction system online, and you're betting on it growing your company for you. Theoretically, that's great. But in your case, it's problematic. You're expecting that system to do all the work for you, so you aren't engaging in other, more traditional prospecting methods. Waiting is not a strategy. In my opinion, waiting is arrogant and lazy. You're resting on your laurels when you haven't even seen any results yet."

If you want to reach new heights, you have to get out of your comfort zone. And don't keep revelling in the "nostalgia of past successes." A past assignment, contract, project or business may have been a huge success, but that doesn't mean you can do it again by following the exact same recipe.

Evolve.

In order to evolve, you need to interact with people who want to help you make progress. Be prepared to hear answers that will make you think and act differently in the future, because once you reach a certain level of success you're going to start hearing more than just praise.

Remember, it's arrogant to believe that past success always guarantees future success.

STOP DOING THINGS HALFWAY

Simon, one of my clients in the food industry, told me that he didn't have enough time to spend with his new employees getting them properly trained. He'd quickly realized that the numerous errors caused by his absence and the inattentive monitoring of company resources were costing the company a lot of money. Even worse, product quality was suffering.

"Simon, you have to apply the following principle: It's urgent that you be rigorous with your time."

Playing catch-up with mistakes is not a winning business strategy.

Your employees don't have clear guidelines, so you can't really blame them. They're irritable, they avoid taking the initiative and they'll be looking for work elsewhere before long.

Cutting corners will eventually cause dissatisfaction among your best clients, and leave you overloaded with tasks that become short-term irritants, affecting your mood and spontaneity in your business relationships.

You don't have to demand perfection, but try not to make YOUR entrepreneurial situation worse. If you only knew how many frustrated entrepreneurs let their situations deteriorate for too long because they aren't thorough enough in their approach.

The downward spiral will only stop if you take the time to start over and do it right, thoroughly and completely, or at least take immediate action to correct what isn't working.

Following my recommendation, Simon started using a smartphone system to film himself preparing each product, and explaining how to do it as part of the video. Then he did the same thing with each of the important procedures that company employees were required to perform.

One video explained how to clean work surfaces, another how to greet customers and answer their questions, a third how to prepare each product, and so on.

The quality of the videos didn't have to be excellent, but employees needed to have quick, easy access the information at all times.

I worked with Kevin, a garage mechanic, to develop *checklists* to ensure that each mechanic performs their tasks properly. The lists have to be signed by the mechanic, which makes them personally responsible for the quality of the job in question. They certify that everything has been done according to best practices. Audits are conducted at random by the garage supervisor. There is no room for error, especially if the employee is committed to quality.

Stop repeating the same things to your employees over and over. Take time now to find the right method for making things work the way they should.

TAKE TIME FOR A RETREAT

Far too many entrepreneurs, and people in general, live like solitary giraffes. They keep their heads bowed so they can peek between their legs and be sure of where they're stepping.

From that position, they can't see the lioness getting ready to pounce, bringing their life to a dramatic end.

Savvy entrepreneurs know they should take a break every year to raise their heads, take note of any potential threats, and choose the right path to achieve their business goals.

Spent at least two days in complete isolation. During that time, start by creating a summary of the past year to consolidate the lessons learned, and then plan your entrepreneurial future. In short, analyze your current situation, and evaluate the coherence of your decisions and actions in terms of your target situation.

Personally, I like to take time during the month of July for this strategic reflection.

I take a detailed look at my situation as an entrepreneur-consultant, then I consider each of my businesses in light of the development initiatives I plan to launch in the coming year. I base the entire analysis on a five-year strategic perspective.

I also evaluate the various opportunities, threats, challenges and blind spots connected to my game plan, and turn it into an action plan with fixed deadlines.

Do I always reach all my goals?

No, because I like to give myself ambitious challenges that are extremely difficult to meet.

Then I show the fruits of my labours to certain trusted individuals, including my mentor, to get an external point of view from someone who isn't directly involved with my operations.

When did you last take a moment to lift your head?

Who can help you see further?

CONCLUSION: YOU'RE RESPONSIBLE FOR EVERYTHING

I would like to conclude this book by reminding you that your entrepreneurial success or failure is entirely up to you. As W.E. Henley says in his poem Invictus, "I am the master of my fate."

You alone are responsible for:

Every decision you make or put off.

Every action you take or delegate.

Every relationship you maintain or neglect.

Every client you serve or turn away.

How quickly you get things done, and how long you make

others wait.

All the people you listen to or push aside.

All the reading that you do or don't do.

The list goes on...

Give yourself a solid whack with a two-by-four every time you feel yourself getting complacent and sitting around. You'll need it to continue growing on a personal level, because entrepreneurship is all about self-discovery and pushing yourself to the limit.

One last thing: Feel free to share what you've read with other entrepreneurs who might need a whack from a two-by-four themselves.

Good luck!

AFTERWORD:
GETTING WHACKED
WITH A
TWO-BY-FOUR HURTS!

Sunday, September 23, 2018, 1:54 a.m.

Like so many entrepreneurs often do, I woke up thinking about an ongoing situation with one of my clients who needs to be challenged more in order for his business to develop.

Since I couldn't go back to sleep, I ended up deciding to quit procrastinating and started working on finalizing some files, including this book. I find that the quiet of nighttime is perfect for working on the kind of project that requires focus.

That explains why I finished writing my new book for entrepreneurs at 4:58 a.m., with my second mug of coffee going cold beside me.

I humbly admit that this has been the most inwardly

and outwardly challenging exercise of my professional career to date.

As you know, I'm used to talking business with entrepreneurs frankly and forcefully, telling it like it is to get them to take action and push them out of complacency.

That said, I've been whacked many times by the figurative two-by-four since the beginning of this writing project last August. Some of my associates challenged me, partners jostled me, some clients gently slapped me upside the head, and François Charron of Votresite.ca really shook me up without realizing it.

I had become what I accuse others of being: reactive instead of proactive.

The situation brought me to what is generally called a crossroads.

A crossroads is a difficult decision we're forced to take that brings us face to face with who we are, which is an uncomfortable position. One path appears on our left, leading to one conclusion, and on our right there's a completely different path with a completely different ending.

Standing in the middle of my crossroads, I had a decision to make and two paths to choose from.

The right thing to do in this kind of situation is usually to take a step back, analyze the situation and make the choice that is most consistent with our vision and objectives.

With everything I needed to get done in the short term, I just didn't have the time and couldn't think quickly enough to make a good strategic decision.

I had to choose between becoming the entrepreneur that I *should* become and the consultant that I *could* become.

How could I continue giving advice to others if I myself was stuck in this situation of duality?

Because I was facing this choice, and it was constantly on my mind, I was less active for a few months.

Wanting to lead by example, I took 24 hours to think exclusively about my situation and discuss it with my mentor, a counsellor and two of my associates.

The reality is that I had gotten too comfortable in the last year (by my own standards), and was refusing to make an important sacrifice because it would distract me from my goals in the short term.

I admit it: I'd fallen fell into the comfort zone trap, that same trap I'm always warning my clients about.

So, for now at least, *Two-by-Four* will be my last book for entrepreneurs.

Since I've chosen to focus on the entrepreneur that I can become, I'm putting all my other writing projects on the back burner and focusing on the growth of my companies. This includes the Clinique d'Accompagnement Entrepreneurial du Québec, which will be making several important announcements in the near future.

I will end this section with a quote from François Charron's preface to my book *Enfin les vraies affaires*, Volume 3:

"Being a good entrepreneur, making the right decisions, developing your entrepreneurial courage (Ouch! It hurts, but it's good for you) and, most importantly, standing on your own two feet, are things that can be learned.

There may even be other Alexandres and François out there with an honest desire to help you grow. Alex, your books and new services make me think that you are becoming the kind of great person that wants to help others become great too."

Becoming a better version of ourselves hurts because it is uncomfortable and uncertain. But it's also necessary.

ACKNOWLEDGEMENTS

I'd like to start by thanking David Couturier and Nicolas Roy for giving me a solid whack with a two-by-four after reading the first draft of this book. They forced me to grow as an author, even though it was uncomfortable and extremely challenging for me. They left me so incredibly frustrated that the final draft of this book was almost postponed indefinitely. That should give you an idea of the impact they had with their feedback.

I want to thank Audrey, my spouse, who greatly facilitates the completion of my projects by picking up the slack at home on a regular basis. Thanks to Zachary and Zoé, my children, who inspire and motivate me to push my limits every day. Seeing my children growing up and discovering the world is fascinating. They are an important part of my success.

Thank you to my business partners, including Johanne Proulx, Nicolas Roy and Michel Ross, who sometimes surprise me with a well-placed whack. Your support is essential to me.

Thank you to my many entrepreneurs who are clients of my companies and the Cellule de Propulsion[MC] program for developing entrepreneurs. You have provided me with countless topics to explore and discuss, and given me several opportunities to put that two-by-four to use.

Thank you to all the people—there are far too many to name—who have given me a taste of my own medicine by throwing me off-balance and making me think again and question the order of things. You've been teaching me to grow by taking action in uncomfortable ways ever since the beginning of my professional career.

These acknowledgements wouldn't be complete without mentioning the enormous influence Yoland Audet and Charles René Lambert have had on me. They have been exceptional mentors and collaborators throughout my business career. Yoland gave me the means to fly very high, while Charles René taught me to go faster by focusing on my natural talents.

Thank you to Myriam Jacob, who I've been lucky enough to have working with me on everything I've written since 2015. She's always the first person to read my books in full before they go to the publishing house. She's always the one who answers first when I ask, "So, what do you think of the book?"

Lastly, I would like to thank the composer Hans Zimmer for his music, which I enjoyed listening to while writing this book. I encourage you to look for his recordings; he's composed the soundtracks to several hit movies.

To me, a company is like an orchestra. Each person

has a well-defined role, and knows exactly which notes to play when to build wonderful harmonies and perform a musical masterpiece. Whenever one member of the ensemble starts thinking they're the star, problems arise. Every member is important to the synergy of the group, even Ringo Starr.

ABOUT THE AUTHOR

Alexandre Vézina

I have a mantra that I regularly share with my clients. It sums up the essence of my philosophy of business, and of life: You are responsible: There is no luck, there are only opportunities that you create for yourself.

Since 2007, I have had the privilege of helping several entrepreneurs from Québec and all over the French-speaking world achieve success. We worked together to tackle questions about management, as well as the challenges that growing companies face.

As an entrepreneur-consultant with many businesses of my own and a passion for discovery, I'm constantly on the lookout for global management trends. I share those trends in concrete terms with other entrepreneurs so that they in turn can apply innovative business models, proven concepts and even unusual new tips.

I use original and varied methods, and I adapt them to each company to provide their leaders with the best possible advice. I provide practical advice and frank opinions. This gives entrepreneurs access to hands-on tools and a realistic perspective on their situation.

My books are filled with concrete ideas, down-to-earth questions and interesting concepts for business development. I encourage you to take a look as well.

To learn more about Alexandre Vézina's services, trainings and conferences, visit www.alexandrevezina.com.

NOTES

[1]Source: *Enfin les vraies affaires*, Volume 3. CHAPTER 51, ATTRACTION ET RÉPULSION (LE PRINCIPE MARILYN MANSON)

[2]Source: blog post at www.alexandrevezina.com.
EN TOUTE HUMILITÉ

[3]Source: *Enfin les vraies affaires*, Volume 2 (book). CHAPTER 52
LE CORRIDOR D'OCCASION AV

[4]Did you know there's a way to buy "likes" and interactions for your company's Facebook posts? That's right, it's because interactions draw other people. In my opinion it's a totally immoral technique, yet many online "experts" use it. Are you going to keep taking advice from someone who's sold their soul to the devil?

[5] I can't believe I have to write this in a book...

[6]Source: *Enfin les vraies affaires*, Volume 1 (book). CHAPTER 2 LE CONCEPT D'ÉQUIVALENCE MENTALE APPLIQUÉ AUX AFFAIRES

[7]Source: *Enfin les vraies affaires*, Volume 1 (book). CHAPTER 2 LE CONCEPT D'ÉQUIVALENCE MENTALE APPLIQUÉ AUX AFFAIRES

[8]Source: *Tout simplement* (book). CHAPTER 11
LA TEINTURE APPLIQUÉE PAR LES AUTRES

[9]Far too many consultants develop business models based on hourly

billing, without considering the results and the actual impact on their clients. They are often employees disguised as entrepreneurs who stick closely to their clients, doing anything and everything just to keep their "job" and billing for as many hours as possible. There are so many other, better alternatives!

[10]   https://en.wikipedia.org/wiki/Muggle

[11]   I honestly can't remember where I learned this trick...

[12]   The term she really used has been changed...

[13]   Reference: *Enfin les vraies affaires*, Volume 2 (book). CHAPTER 20 N'ACCEPTEZ PAS TROP DE *YES MEN* DANS VOTRE ENTOURAGE !

www.ingramcontent.com/pod-product-compliance
Lightning Source LLC
LaVergne TN
LVHW050904200726
843508LV00011B/2106